NON LEAGUE FOOTBALL IN SCOTLAND (EAST)

Perth and Fife

By Andy McGregor

Rel8 Media, 2007

Non League Football in Scotland (East) Perth and Fife

Published by Rel8 Media
PO Box 29145, Dunfermline, Fife, KY12 7WJ

© Rel8 Media and Andy McGregor, 2007

All rights reserved. No part of this publication may be reproduced or copied in any manner without the permission of the copyright holders. A great deal of effort has been made to ensure that the information in this book is as accurate as possible. However, the publishers or author cannot accept responsibility for any consequences arising from using this book.

Sources used have been credited where appropriate and we apologise should we have neglected to include the source of any item.

British Library in Publication Data.
A catalogue record for this volume is available from the British Library.

ISBN 978-0-9555307-0-8

CONTENTS

Page 6	Non League Football in Scotland—Explained?
Page 8	A Junior A-Z
Page 11	The League Structure in Fife and Perthshire
Page 12	Ballingry Rovers
Page 16	Bankfoot Athletic
Page 19	Crossgates Primrose
Page 23	Former Junior Football Venues in the Fife Area
Page 24	Dundonald Bluebell
Page 28	Glenrothes
Page 33	Hill of Beath Hawthorn
Page 38	Jeanfield Swifts
Page 42	Former Junior Football Ground sin the Perth Area
Page 43	Kelty Hearts
Page 47	Kinnoull
Page 51	Kirkcaldy YM
Page 54	Lochgelly Albert
Page 59	Lochore Welfare
Page 63	Luncarty
Page 66	Newburgh
Page 70	Oakley United
Page 73	Rosyth
Page 78	Scone Thistle
Page 82	St Andrew's United
Page 86	Steelend Victoria
Page 89	Thornton Hibs
Page 93	Burntisland Shipyard
Page 97	Amateur Football

ACKNOWLEDGEMENTS

Much of what is written about football, including what is in this book, is drawn from other published sources. Some of the information in this book is drawn from primary research. There is a scarcity of published material about Scottish Junior football but there are a number of publications that have been consulted in the compilation of this book and should be acknowledged. The *Scottish Non League Review* has been published by S Davidson in Renfrewshire since the late 1980s and faithfully chronicles the various league and cup results. The same publisher also produced a number of booklets of *Scottish Non League Histories* which are valuable sources of information. Eric R Thomson's *'Fields of Fife'*, published privately circa 1990 details all of the football grounds of the Kingdom and was another valuable source. Paul Crankshaw published a booklet of *Scottish Junior Cup* results covering 1968 until 1989, and Stewart Davidson produced a similar work for the years 1960-1968. Both have been consulted in compiling this book. The *Scottish Football Historian,* edited by John Litster, ha sbeen published quarterly since the 1980s and has provided some material. Two publications by David Allan have also been helpful—*Fifeshire Football Memories* and *There Was A Happyland* (a history of football in Lochgelly). *The Winners*, published in 2004 by Bernard Stocks is an invaluable source for lists of competition winners an details. Various club websites and programmes, too numerous to mention individually, have also been consulted.

COVER PICTURES—Clockwise from top right, show the Warout Stadium in Glenrothes, Simpson Park in Perth, Lochore Welfare v Pollok 2006/7 and Recreation Park in Rosyth.

All pictures in this book were taken by the Author.

NON LEAGUE FOOTBALL IN SCOTLAND—EXPLAINED?

To the outsider it can be very difficult to fathom the structure of non-league football in Scotland. Terms such as Junior, Senior, Amateur and Juvenile are confusing and there seem to be so many layers and regions of organised football.

The two most important levels of non-league football north of the border are Junior and Senior football. Despite the nomenclature there is no age-specific distinction between these grades of football.

The Scottish Junior FA comprises more than 150 clubs who form an almost totally self-contained level of football. The Juniors are organised into three main regions—North (Aberdeen and the areas to the North and West), East (Angus, Perthshire, Fife, Edinburgh and the Lothians) and West (Glasgow, Lanarkshire, Renfrewshire, Dunbartonshire and Ayrshire). Each of the three regions has a 'Super League' competition. East and West also have a 'Premier League', a sort of Super League Division 2. Beneath these are more localised Leagues. The only national competition is the Scottish Junior Cup, played on a knock-out basis between all member clubs. Traditionally Junior clubs have not been full members of the Scottish Football Association and are therefore ineligible to play in the Scottish Cup itself, although that situation is more fluid now than ever before.

Senior non-league football does not have a national governing body of its own. There are three main Leagues—the Highland League, East of Scotland League and South of Scotland League. Many of the members of these leagues, but not all, are full members of the Scottish Football Association and are eligible to play in the Scottish Cup. Some members of the East and South Leagues are not full SFA members. There is a further 'senior' league for clubs to the north of Inverness, known as the North Caledonian League, but only one team (Golspie) is a full SFA member.

There is no national Senior non-league competition. SFA member teams from the East and South have traditionally played in the Scottish Qualifying Cup (South) and those from the North have played, unsurprisingly, in the Scottish Qualifying Cup (North).

The spheres of influence of the seniors and juniors are almost mutually exclusive. The far south-west of Scotland is a senior area. Clubs there are members of the South of Scotland League and there are no junior teams. The same is true of the Borders where teams are members of the senior East of Scotland League.. The City of Edinburgh has just one Junior team with the remainder of the top non-league clubs being Seniors. However, Edinburgh's hinterland of the Lothian counties is predominantly a Junior stronghold. West Central Scotland is almost exclusively Junior, along with Ayrshire, Fife, Dundee and Angus. Only in the Eastern Highlands, where the Highland League exists alongside the North Juniors, do the two levels co-inhabit the same areas.

Scottish football has no meaningful ground grading system and this creates several anomalies. Clubs wishing to join the SFA over recent decades have had to satisfy very strict ground criteria. However, current members are allowed to retain their status even if their ground is well below the standards required of new clubs. Consequently the likes of Coldstream and Civil Service Strollers play in the Scottish Qualifying Cup each year, despite having roped off pitches in what amount to public parks and playing fields. Junior clubs are required to have enclosed grounds but the concept of seating is almost entirely alien to the culture of Junior football. A few Junior clubs have very presentable grounds with seating, cover and all-round spectator comforts but they are very much the exception.

Floodlights are universal in the Highland League and midweek fixtures are scheduled there. Although some Junior clubs have lights they are not used for competitive matches—meaning Saturdays only from September to March, and early kick offs for mid winter games.

The great divide between Senior and Juniors is starting to show some signs of crumbling. The first club to bridge the gap was Girvan FC from South Ayrshire. They switched from the Senior South of Scotland League to the higher-standard Ayrshire Junior League, but retained their SFA membership. They became the first club of modern times to play in both the Scottish Qualifying Cup and the Scottish Junior Cup in the same season. Banks o' Dee, from Aberdeen, a long-standing Junior club, joined the senior Aberdeenshire FA to play in local senior Cups although they have not yet joined the Scottish FA.

In 2006 plans were put forward for four Junior clubs to compete in the Scottish Cup proper from 2007/8. The idea is to scrap the senior Qualifying Cup competition and have an all-in tournament with teams from different levels joining at various stages. The Champions of the North, East and West Super Leagues, as well as the Scottish Junior Cup winners, would enter the following season's Scottish Cup. Existing SFA members from the Senior non leagues would continue to enter the Scottish Cup. If a team won the East or South Senior Leagues that was not an SFA member, which is quite possible, then they would also gain a place in the Scottish Cup for the following season. This proposal will be voted on in June 2007.

What then of the other levels of non-league football in Scotland? Juvenile football is age-specific. Various leagues exist in different parts of the country although the quality of juvenile football clubs has declined. One of the reasons for this is that many senior clubs now run their own youth teams in ring-fenced youth leagues, creaming off the better players. However, Juvenile clubs, sometimes known by the very non p.c. term of Boys Clubs, are still playing football around the country from under 21 level down to Under 8 and Under 9. At one time there were Under 27 teams although they disappeared many years ago. Juvenile clubs, almost without exception, play on public parks and playing fields.

Amateur football thrives across the whole country. Again it is played mainly on public parks but a few clubs have their own enclosed grounds. The annual Scottish Amateur Cup involves upwards of 800 sides. There are local Amateur Leagues in most counties. There are also several leagues that cover a wider area, although non are truly national. Several competing leagues span the Edinburgh and Glasgow areas as well as Stirlingshire and beyond. The Caledonian Amateur Football League and Central Scottish Amateur League are the strongest, with teams in membership across the Central Belt. The Scottish Amateur League, despite its name, is restricted in membership to the Glasgow area and the West.

Strong and competitive Amateur FAs exist in the Borders, Fife, Stirlingshire, Perthshire, Dundee and Angus, Aberdeen and in the North.

Some senior clubs run 'second teams' in Amateur competitions. The only remaining 'Senior' club whose first team are in the Amateurs is Burntisland Shipyard AFC of the Fife League. They have retained SFA membership since the 1930s and continue to play in the Qualifying Cup every year.

The only other level of football in Scotland is Welfare Football. Even this is far from simple—some Welfare FAs play Summer competitions and others play Winter competitions. It may be inaccurate and unkind to brand the Winter Welfare teams as belonging to 'pub leagues' but it may also be the best way to encapsulate what winter welfare is about. The Summer Leagues are mainly in the North with the exception of the Forth and Endrick League in West Stirlingshire and Dunbartonshire. The Summer leagues are generally of a higher standard than their winter counterparts.

A JUNIOR A-Z

ATTENDANCES
Official attendances are seldom given. St Andrew's and Rosyth give crowd figures in their match programmes. These reveal that crowds across the region seldom deviate from the 50-150 mark. What is noticeable about attendances at junior games is that the crowds are predominantly male and predominantly mature. This does not augur well for the future of football at this level. Generally poor facilities make many grounds an unattractive proposition and particularly for women and children.

CATERING
It is very unusual for a Junior game to take place without food and drinks being on sale to those attending. Kirkcaldy YM rely on the appearance of a van in the street outside the ground – otherwise clubs have their own catering facilities of varying quality. At Steelend regulars have their own china mugs; at St Andrew's the choice is awesome although the facility tends not to open until nearly half time; at Ballingry the facilities are excellent. The ubiquitous Scotch Pie dominates the menu. It is possible that sausage rolls, bridies or steak pies may also be available. Chocolate bars, chewy sweets and crisps are pretty standard. Drinks-wise every club will offer at least Bovril and tea. Coffee may be an option or may not. Soft drinks usually come in the can. Prices are generally very reasonable – less than half what one would pay at the likes of Dunfermline Athletic or St Johnstone. For vegetarians the choice is limited, usually to the apple you'll have brought with you.

COMPETITIONS
The multitude of Cup competitions means that every club has at least half-a-dozen opportunities to land some silverware each season. Fixture congestion means that most Cups do not deal in replays any more. In fact, only the Scottish Junior Cup has scheduled replays, and at the end of these ties will be decided on penalties. In domestic cups some games go straight to penalties after 90 minutes and some have extra time first. It can be very hard to keep track of local Cups from year to year—most change heir name according to which sponsor in on board at the time.

ENTRANCE
Turnstiles are not a feature of most junior grounds. Payment is made at a table or pay-box on entry to the ground. In most cases you will be given a ticket which, in theory, serves as a pass out should you wish to leave the ground at some point. At

some grounds it is possible to manage a quick pint in a nearby pub during the half time interval. The gate checker will remain on duty until the stroke of half time – you'll be expected to pay up until then. After that you can see the second half for free if you want. Admission in 2006/7 was generally £4 but major Cup ties could be a fiver. Most gatemen do not take kindly to being presented with twenty pound notes. Try and have a pocketful of change before turning up.

FIXTURE LISTS
The concept of a whole-season fixture list in Junior football simply does not exist. The dates for the various rounds of the Scottish Junior Cup are decided pre-season but that as far as it goes for pre-planning. It is likely that early season fixtures, up to mid September, will be available from the start of the season. After that it really is a week-to-week basis – fixtures can usually be found on the internet from the previous Sunday. The best sites to look at are the East Region website, the unofficial 'Not The Pink News' site and the various club sites. The Fife Referees Association site can also be useful for checking fixtures at various levels—look under 'Appointments' to see what is coming up.

East Region—http://www.ultrasoft.hostinguk.com/ersjfa
Not The Pink News—http://www.ultrasoft.hostinguk.com/Arniston2/Pink.asp
Fife Referees— http://www.fifereferees.co.uk/index.htm

KICK OFF TIMES
Even in high summer, and some teams will still be playing then, Saturday kick off times are 2.30pm at the latest. In mid winter kick off times creep forward, and Cup ties with the potential for extra time or penalties can kick off as early as 1pm. Midweek games are restricted to August and maybe the first week of September, and from early April onwards. Depending on the time of year the scheduled kick off time for these can vary from 6.15pm to 7.15pm. Even teams that have floodlights almost never use them for matches. Hill of Beath and Ballingry have been known to switch them on but only if the evening is unexpectedly dark. During the midweek rush to complete fixtures games will often start once the teams have turned up – players arriving from work will frequently screech into the car park ten minutes prior to kick off.

NEWSPAPER COVERAGE
For information about Junior football in this part of the world the best coverage is in Dundee's Daily Newspaper, the Courier. Two regional editions are produced – one covering Fife and one for Perthshire. The Fife edition, sold throughout the Kingdom, has good coverage on Monday, Friday and Saturday. Kinross and Milnathort are good places for being able to buy both editions. The Edinburgh Evening News covers the Super League and Premier League but has very little on the Central Division clubs – the Monday and Friday editions are the ones to check out. The various local weekly newspapers cover their local sides – the Perthshire Advertiser, Dunfermline Press and Fife Free Press (Kirkcaldy) all cover a number of sides. The other even more local and parochial papers provide additional coverage for some clubs.

PLAYING STANDARDS
Taking the Scottish Premier League, Scottish Football League, Highland, East and South Senior Leagues and the various Junior sides there are around 250 teams

taking the field each week in Scottish non-league football. The standard in the Juniors varies greatly. Top sides such as Hill of Beath, Kelty and Kinnoull would challenge the best of the Highland League and possibly the Third Division of the SFL. The sides towards the bottom of the East Central League, such as Newburgh and Steelend, are some distance away from this. Drawing a comparison with England might be useful—if Scotland has 250 teams for 5 million people, then they must span the quality range of the top 2500 teams in England. In effect that means from the Premiership right down to Level 7 of the Pyramid. A few of the top Junior sides, drawing crowds of up to a couple of hundred, might be commensurate with Level 3 of the English system—the Unibond, Isthmian and Southern Leagues. But the majority of Junior teams are more in line with levels 6 and 7 of the English pyramid, drawing crowds of a few dozen. Where the Scottish clubs lag far behind is in terms of facilities. Whilst the majority of English non-league grounds, even at Levels 5 and below, are well-maintained, have floodlights and vibrant social clubs or pavilions, these are the exception for equivalent clubs in Scotland.

PROGRAMMES

A few clubs are diligent in the production of programmes and have been for a number of years. Super League Kinnoull, Premier League St Andrew's United and Scone Thistle and Central Division Rosyth can reasonably be relied upon to produce programmes for home games. Glenrothes of the Premier League also started producing programmes early in 2006/7. These stalwarts aside, it is difficult to predict with any certainty if a programme will be on sale for any given game. The production of a programme is often down to the enthusiasm of one individual and if their enthusiasm wanes then the programme will cease publication. Kirkcaldy YM, for instance, issued for every game for a couple of years but stopped as quickly as they had started. Scottish Junior Cup ties usually elicit programmes at the likes of Kelty Hearts and Hill of Beath, who also issue for some other games. Forget the notion of phoning up in advance to find out if there will be a programme for a game – the club secretary may have no idea until the day of the match whether or not someone has put together a programme. A frequent explanation for no programme being on sale is that 'the guy who does it isn't here today'. The pool of enthusiasts available to support Junior clubs is small and the development of websites has, in some instances, been detrimental to programme production.

RAFFLE

The half-time raffle is omnipresent in junior football. It is customary to buy £1 worth of tickets – failure to do so may cause offence! Tickets are usually proffered by a seller at the entrances – someone may also circumnavigate the whole ground during the first half to sell tickets. It is usually the referee who makes the draw at the start of half time – the winning tickets will either be paraded around the ground on a board, or pinned to a noticeboard near the entrances. You will nor retire on your winnings, but you may end up with a sore head. The presence of the raffle is another reason why some clubs are ambivalent to programmes – they believe that programmes will undermine raffle sales.

SOUVENIRS

Very few clubs sell much in the way of souvenirs. Some have produced badges, or had badges produced for them, but few still have them on sale. Committee men might be wearing a club tie or badge but these tend to be a 'badge of office' rather than something that is available to the general public. Reaching a Scottish Cup Final or Semi Final usually prompts the appearance of a range of scarves and hats and the occasional replica strip for sale.

SEATING
Grandstands and junior football do not normally go together. A few grounds in the Fife and Perth areas do have small areas of seating but this is the exception rather than the norm. Glenrothes have an excellent stand in their municipally-owned stadium. At the other end of the scale Newburgh have a quirky little seated stand dating back many years.

TOILETS
Extremely variable. Most grounds will have a lean-to of some description which serves as a urinal. In some cases this may even be connected to mains water and sewerage. For more serious business it may be necessary to enquire at the pavilion. Ladies are not always catered for in the time warp world of junior football, although club officials will usually arrange for access to the pavilion if required.

THE LEAGUE STRUCTURE IN FIFE AND PERTHSHIRE

Junior Football has undergone various stages of reconstruction down the years. Until 1968 junior football was arranged by 'county'. Perthshire and Fife both had their own Junior associations and ran league and cup competitions. In 1968 a series of 'regions' was created—North, Tayside, Fife, Lothians, Central and Ayrshire. Fife was by far the smallest of these and managed to retain 'independence' when others disappeared. Nothing much changed until the early 2000s when the 'Super Regions' were created—the new 'East Region' embraced the former Tayside, Fife and Lothians regions. An East 'Super League' of 12 clubs was established with subsidiary Tayside, Fife and Lothians Leagues. The champions of each of these were promoted to the Super League at the end of each season. For 2006/7 a second level 'Premier Division' was established, also of 12 teams. Almost without realising it the Juniors were creating a 'pyramid structure' all of their own.

The creation of the Premier League left the Fife League looking very short of teams. To improve the balance of clubs the Tayside, Fife and Lothians divisions were replaced by North, Central and South divisions, and the Perthshire Junior clubs switched from the Tayside to the Central Division. In terms of travelling this made little difference to them—it may be correct to say that they will have shorter distances to travel along better roads allowing for faster journeys. Coupar Angus and Blairgowrie, one time members of the Perthshire Association remain in the North with only the Perth-based and 'west of Tay' clubs switching.

The problem with the present structure is that there is no chance of progression beyond it. The pyramid ends with the East Super League. Of course most Junior clubs are quite happy with that and would not want to go further but there are some clubs that are genuinely ambitious. The Scottish Football League remains a 'closed shop' and the best and most forward-looking Junior clubs can only look enviously at the fully-developed pyramid structure in England.

BALLINGRY ROVERS

Ground—Ore Park, Glencraig
Ground Phone Number—01592 868516
Postcode / GPS Location –KY5 8AB

Club Colours— Tangerine and Black

Club Secretary 2006/7—Edward Easson, 01592 748778

Stand by to be confused! The geography of football in this area of Fife is very complex. Lochgelly Albert, Ballingry Rovers and Lochore Welfare all play within three miles of each other in Central Fife. Lochgelly Albert do play in Lochgelly. Ballingry Rovers do not play in Ballingry—their home is at Ore Park in Glencraig. Lochore Welfare do not play in Lochore—their Central Park ground is in Crosshill. The nearest ground to Lochgelly Railway Station is Ballingry's. There is a junior-standard football ground in Ballingry which was home to Benarty, a team that had one season at Junior level in 1998/9. It is now used by Benarty Amateurs, twice winners of the Fife Amateur Cup in the 1990s.

HISTORY
Football has been played in Glencraig since at least the 1890s. A junior team called Glencraig Celtic existed briefly during the late Victorian era. They folded quickly and a side called Glencraig Rangers emerged, playing at North End Park. Their star shone only briefly around 1903 and 1904. Later, in 1908, another team called Glencraig Celtic took up the mantle for local football players, playing out of Bore Park, a few hundred metres south of North End Park. The Celtic met their demise in 1926. They were followed by another junior team called Glencraig Colliery who benefited from sponsorship and support from the coal industry—teams that adopted the suffix Colliery were eligible for special grants and subsidies. The Colliery team was formed in 1938 and played until 1956.

The demise of Glencraig Colliery Juniors coincides with the formation of Ballingry Rovers. They spent season 1956/7 in the Junior game before stepping down to Amateur status.

Ballingry Rovers are relative newcomers to the Junior ranks. Although the club was formed in 1956, after their one season at Junior level they remained in Amateur football until 2004 when they again stepped up to the Junior ranks. As an Amateur side they won the Fife Amateur Cup on 4 occasions and enjoyed considerable success in other local competitions. They also reached the Final of the Scottish Amateur Cup in 1980.

Ballingry found the step up to Junior level challenging but they eventually made some progress. It took them until March 2005 to win a game but after that they never looked back. Five more league victories followed allowing a respectable mid-table finish.

It was not until 2006/7 that Ballingry recorded their first Scottish Junior Cup success. They reached Round Four before losing to Glasgow club Petershill in a replay which was played at Dunipace because of ground works at Petershill. 2006/7 also brought some success in local Cups with a notable win over Super League side Bonnyrigg Rose and a draw against Linlithgow Rose.

GROUND
Ore Park, home of Ballingry Rovers, lies on or very close to the site of North End Park, the field used by Glencraig Rangers in Edwardian times. Coincident with their rise to Junior level, Ballingry have completed some major ground improvements. The park is one of the better-appointed grounds in the East Juniors.

Entering through the gates on Clune Terrace, situated level with the half way line, there are small covered enclosures to either side. To the west end is the sizeable catering outlet—a large and unusually clean establishment offering a wider range of pies and burgers than is typical at this level. Behind the west goal is a small seated grandstand. The north and east sides of the ground are flat standing. Some parts are concrete hard standing so spectators are less likely to get filthy in this ground than in many others.

Outside the ground, across Clune Terrace, is a large building which houses the changing rooms and social club facilities. As is typical at most junior grounds there is a wall-display of pennants from clubs that Ballingry have met down the years,

Rovers are very proud of their role as a community Sports and Social club. The Bar and Function area provides entertainment for members throughout the year. There is also a gym and fitness area which is available to members. Match sponsors are catered for with their own lounge with bar facilities.

Ballingry have a floodlight system that is reckoned to be good enough for midweek fixtures, but as it stands opponents are not obliged to play under them. Winter matches will kick off early, and midweek games are restricted to early and late season.

There is no doubting the ambition of this club. They tried a bold experiment in Sunday football by switching their local derby against Lochore Welfare to Christmas Eve 2006 and were rewarded with a bumper crowd. The game went ahead despite foggy conditions thanks, in part, to the floodlighting system.

SUPPORT
Ballingry Rovers have worked very hard to create interest in the club. Their facilities are amongst the best in the area. Despite the fact that few people live close to the ground they do have a hard core of a hundred or so spectators.

GETTING THERE
If anyone wants to be brave and take the train then Lochgelly station is not too far away from the ground. It's about 15 minutes walk away, all downhill on the way to the ground, and uphill on the way back! Lochgelly is on the Fife Circle service from Edinburgh—take the trains going to Dunfermline and Cowdenbeath rather than those for Kirkcaldy to get there quicker. You could go one way and back the other if you want to complete the 'Fife Circle' which takes you through some of the great

names of Scottish League and Non-League football—Rosyth, Dunfermline, Cowdenbeath, Lochgelly, Glenrothes, Thornton, Kirkcaldy and Burntisland to name but some of them.

Car parking is no problem for typical matches at Ore Park. For bigger games it may be necessary to bump up onto the verge of the main road (the B920) passing the ground. The easiest way to reach Glencraig by road is from the Lochgelly exit from the A92(T) road from Dunfermline (Halbeath) to Glenrothes. Follow the Lochgelly signs from the A92, and take a left at the second roundabout. This leads to the centre of Lochgelly, such as it is. At the 'T' Junction take a right, heading for Lochore and Ballingry. Pass the High School on the left and the ground is then visible a few hundred yards further on, to the left.

PROGRAMMES
Ballingry are reputed to produce programmes for some games although they are few and far between. In 2005 they certainly issued an excellent programme when they hosted a local Cup Final between Hill of Beath and Kirkcaldy YM.

WEBSITE
The club website can be found at:
www.ballingryrovers.co.uk/
The site does not always appear to be updated on a regular basis.

TEN YEAR LEAGUE RECORD

| 2004/5 | Fife League | 8th out of 12 | 23pts |
| 2005/6 | Fife League | 7th out of 13 | 30 pts |

THE TOWN
Glencraig is now little more than a row of houses on the main road between Lochgelly and Crosshill. The demise of the coal mining industry brought the demolition of the miner's rows which used to comprise most of the village. One of these was known as Clune Terrace and was located where the preset day road to the ground leads off the main road. The Collieries themselves were on the eastern side of the main road. Access was via the farm road that now leads to Inchgall Farm. The adjacent settlements of Lochore, Crosshill, Ballingry and Lochgelly are amongst the most deprived in the whole of Scotland. Ballingry, which means Village of the Cave in Gaelic, still elects a councillor to Fife Council who although nominally an Independent, is in fact a Communist —probably one of the last places in Europe to do so! The gap left by the ending of coal mining has never really been filled in this area—unemployment is high. There are numerous pubs and clubs in Lochgelly, Lochore and Ballingry but they do not look too enticing for visitors. This impression may, of course, be totally misleading. Lochgelly has a sprinkling of shops but there is very little within walking distance of Ballingry Rovers ground. Ballingry itself was built in the 1950s and early 1960s as a 'green field' housing scheme to replace the squalid miners rows of the Benarty area. There is a certain 'symmetry' in the fact that Ballingry Rovers play on the site of Glencraig Village—the tightly packed miner's rows that once stood there were replaced with the 'housing of the future' in Ballingry, and the population moved a couple of miles up the road.

SCOTTISH JUNIOR CUP RECORD

04/5	Rd 1	H	Wishaw	1-3
05/6	Rd 1	Bye		
	Rd 2	A	Rosyth Recreation	2-4
06/7	Rd 1	Bye		
	Rd 2	A	RAF Lossiemouth	5-0
	Rd 3	A	Haddington Athletic	2-0
	Rd 4	H	Petershill	1-1
	Rep	A	Petershill	0-1

HONOURS

Since returning to Junior football in 2004, Ballingry Rovers have not won any Cups or Championships. Given the ambition that is evident at the club this situation might change soon.

TOP PICTURE—It looks as if the Social Club building is in the ground but in fact there is a street between the standing area and the building. Ballingry's dressing rooms are in another building to the right of the Social Club. These fans are congregated in this corner of the ground, not for the great view, but for a quick getaway to beat the half-time queue at the bar.

LOWER PICTURE —Ore Park is a bit of a 'hotch potch' of different enclosures and stands. The east end has a seated stand behind the goal complete with red plastic seats. The structure in the foreground houses the announcer—this is one of the few grounds with a functioning Public Address system. Behind the perimeter wall the club are developing a training area.

BANKFOOT ATHLETIC

Ground—Coronation Park, Bankfoot
Ground Phone Number—
Postcode / GPS Location – PH1 4BQ

Club Colours— Maroon and White

Club Secretary 2006/7—Stuart Angus, 01738 622744

HISTORY
Bankfoot Athletic were formed in 1919. Initially they were a Juvenile club but in 1922 they moved up to Junior level. However, after two seasons they reverted to the Juveniles and remained there until 1946. Although neighbouring villages such as Stanley, Luncarty and Dunkeld had teams in the Perthshire Senior League down the years, Bankfoot always restricted themselves to Junior and Juvenile football.

One of the best players ever-produced by Bankfoot Athletic was striker Paul Sturrock who went on to play for Dundee United and Scotland. Later, as a manager, he enjoyed success with St Johnstone, Dundee United, Plymouth Argyle and Sheffield Wednesday. He had a less successful spell in charge of Southampton and more recently was boss of Swindon Town.

Honours have seldom gone the way of Bankfoot. As a Junior side it took them from 1946 until 1973 to get their name on a trophy - the short-lived John Masson Cup. Apart from that the only Cup they have won is the Winter Cup, for lower league Tayside clubs, on one occasion. For a spell at the end of the 1990s they yo-yoed between the two Tayside divisions before sinking almost without trace in the early 2000s.

They have had very little success in the Scottish Junior Cup, seldom progressing beyond the Second Round.

The club operate a team at Under 12 level in the local juvenile league. They also play at Coronation Park, usually on Sundays. Perhaps due to the enthusiasm of parents and friends, the juvenile team seem to get more publicity that their junior counterparts.

GROUND
Coronation Park is situated in Newhall Street in Bankfoot. There are no real spectator facilities at the ground. A small pavilion stands on one side of the pitch but as far as the rest goes it is just grass roped off from the playing field. This is one of those grounds that stretches the Scottish Junior FA's definition of 'enclosed' to the limit. Rule 6 of the SJFA's Cup Tie Rules stats that any ground used for a Scottish Junior Cup tie must "efficiently prevents the public having access thereto without payment and has dressing accommodation, including full toilet and washing facilities for the teams of each club within the ground."

SUPPORT
The villagers of Bankfoot do not really get out to support their team. For a typical match a 'home' crowd of a dozen or so would be regarded as normal.

GETTING THERE
Bankfoot is located a few miles north of Perth. It used to be on the old A9 road from Perth to Inverness but since the 1970s it has been 'by-passed' by the new A9. Travelling by road from Perth, Bankfoot is signposted from the A9. This takes the driver into the southern end of the village. As you approach the centre of the village turn left into Prieston Road and then take the second right into Newhall Street. It might be more advisable to park in Prieston Road because Newhall Street is narrow and usually impossible to park in because of residents and players. In the event of coming from the north the Bankfoot exit from the A9 is several miles from the village, close to Dunkeld. Follow the Bankfoot signs through Waterloo to approach Bankfoot, turning right at the far end of the main street into Prieston Road.

Rail travellers will find that Dunkeld is the nearest station although Perth has a better range of rail services. Dunkeld is on the main Perth to Inverness line.

Stagecoach Bus Service 23 from Perth to Aberfeldy passes trough both Bankfoot and Dunkeld. Journey time from Perth is 30 minutes, and from Dunkeld 10 minutes - frequency is approximately two-hourly.

PROGRAMMES
Bankfoot Athletic have issued programmes at various times but are not thought to have done so in the past few seasons. Collectors might be able to get their hands on special issues for their pre-season tournament in the 1990s, as well as some league issues from around the same time.

WEBSITE
The Bankfoot Athletic website used to be located at:
http://www.bajfc.com/
Sadly it appears to be permanently 'down'. It used to be one of the best Junior club websites in the area.

TEN YEAR LEAGUE RECORD

1996/7	Tayside League Div One	13th out of 14	21pts	Relegated
1997/8	Tayside League Div Two	4th out of 11	38pts	
1998/9	Tayside League 1st Div	1st out of 12	45pts	Promoted
1999/0	Tayside Premier League	11th out of 12	16pts	Relegated
2000/1	Tayside League 1st Div	1st out of 12	49pts	Promoted
2001/2	Tayside Premier League	11th out of 12	22pts	Relegated
2002/3	Tayside League 1st Div	10th out of 10	4pts	
2003/4	Tayside League 1st Div	8th out of 10	19pts	
2004/5	Tayside League 1st Div	7th out of 10	22pts	
2005/6	Tayside League 1st Div	6th out of 9	15pts	

TOWN (Population 1004)
Bankfoot has a population of approximately 1000. The village was established in 1815 at the time of road improvements – it lay on the new turnpike between Perth and Dunkeld. The neighbouring village of Waterloo was created at the same time. At one time a passenger-carrying Light Railway linked Bankfoot to the main line at Luncarty. This closed to passengers in the 1930s but remained open for freight (mainly tatties) until the 1960s. In the early 1970s the village was by-passed by new improvements to the A9, improving the quality of life for residents significantly. Adjacent to the village, just off the A9, is the Perthshire Visitor Centre. Basically this is a retail outlet specialising in Scottish souvenirs and produce. Also located here are the Scottish Liqueur Centre and the MacBeth Experience.

SCOTTISH JUNIOR CUP RECORD

88/9	Rd 1	Bye		
	Rd 2	A	Benburb	1-2
89/90	Rd 1	Bye		
	Rd 2	H	Penicuik Athletic	0-2
90/1	Rd 1	H	Dundee North End	0-2
91/2	Rd 1	Bye		
	Rd 2	A	Glencairn	1-4
92/3	Rd 1	H	Dyce	2-0
	Rd 2	H	Lesmahagow	1-6
93/4	Rd 1	Bye		
	Rd 2	H	Kilwinning Rangers	2-6
94/5	Rd 1	Bye		
	Rd 2	A	Thornton Hibs	8-2
	Rd 3	H	Aberdeen Lad Club	1-2
95/6	Rd 1	Bye		
	Rd 2	A	Cumnock	0-9
96/7	Rd1	A	Arbroath Vics	2-0
	Rd2	H	Musselburgh Athle	0-2
97/8	Rd 1	Bye		
	Rd 2	A	Carluke Rovers	1-1
	Rep	H	Carluke Rovers	2-1
	Rd 3	A	Vale of Leven	1-2
98/9	Rd 1	Bye		
	Rd 2	A	Buckie Rovers	4-3
	Rd 3	H	Stoneyburn	1-1
	Rep	A	Stoneyburn	2-3
99/0	Rd 1	H	Longside	3-2
	Rd 2	A	Cruden Bay	3-3
	Rep	H	Cruden Bay	2-1
	Rd 3	A	Pollok	0-3
00/1	Rd 1	Bye		
	Rd 2	A	Dalry Thistle	1-2
01/2	Rd 1	H	Scone Thistle	1-2
02/3	Rd 1	H	Newburgh	0-4
03/4	Rd 1	Bye		
	Rd 2	H	Forfar Albion	1-4
04/5	Rd 1	A	Vale of Clyde	1-2
05/6	Rd 1	Bye		
	Rd 2	A	Dalry Thistle	0-5
06/7	Rd 1	H	Hill of Beath H	2-6

TOP PHOTO shows the public park surroundings of Coronation Park in Bankfoot.

LOWER PHOTO shows the pavilion and, in the foreground, the seated accommodation (Capacity 3, or 4 if the folk are wee).

These pictures were taken more than ten years ago but little has changed in that time

HONOURS

Tayside Regional League Division 2 -
1983/4, 1998/9, 2000/1
John Masson Cup - 1973/4

CROSSGATES PRIMROSE

Ground—Humbug Park, Crossgates
Ground Phone Number—
Postcode / GPS Location – KY4 8AT

Club Colours— Primrose Yellow and Blue

Club Secretary 2006/7— Derrick Easton, 01383 612038

Junior football clubs often adopt floral names which may or may not bear some relation to their club colours. In the case of Crossgates Primrose, the flower is reflected in their choice of yellow jerseys.

HISTORY
Organised football has been played in the village of Crossgates since at least the 1880s. The first prominent team from the village was Crossgates Thistle, who played in Fife junior competitions from 1906. They originally played at a ground called Allan Park, to the north of the village, but by 1911 they had moved to Humbug Park. The 1913 Ordnance Survey map reveals that embankments had been created for spectator viewing.

Some sources give a date of foundation for Crossgates Primrose of 1927. However, the club website gives 1926 as the date. Whatever, they were successful relatively quickly, winning the Cowdenbeath Cup in 1928/9. In 1933 Humbug Park was substantially upgraded. Primrose had to move out for a year while work was carried out and they played their games at Schoolview Park, adjacent to the present Primary School buildings.

Primrose purchased the revamped Humbug Park for the sum of £65. It was regarded as one of the best grounds in Fife at the time and was used for several local Cup finals.

The Crossgates side of the early 1950s was their most successful. In 1952/3 they reached the 6th Round of the Scottish Junior Cup - a feat that has not been equalled since. The Cup run attracted massive attendances at Humbug Park. Different sources quote various figures for these games but going by the club website a crowd of 7600 packed into Humbug Park for the 5th Round tie against Auchinleck Talbot, with 4485 against Annbank United (Round 6) and 5000 against Blantyre Victoria in an earlier round. The club purchased 400 railway sleepers to make terracing around the field. Around this time the ground was also used for Greyhound racing.

As often happens in Junior football the fortunes of a club can fluctuate very quickly. By 1960 Primrose had folded and Humbug Park lay vacant. The ground was sold to Dunfermline Athletic for £900. Pars boss Jock Stein, always far-sighted and ahead of his time, reckoned that Dunfermline Athletic needed their own training ground. The Pars re-aligned the pitch by turning it 90 degrees and built a caretakers house in the grounds. Although the club had ceased playing in 1960 they remained extant as a social and pools club. In 1983 they made a welcome return to junior football, again using Humbug Park as their home. By this time Dunfermline had sold the ground to the local council. The first match back as a junior club was on 13th August 1983 when Dundonald Bluebell were defeated 3-1 at Humbug Park.

Over the years Primrose have provided a number of players for senior football. Local side Dunfermline Athletic have benefited from the likes of John Lunn, Willie Callaghan and Willie Cunningham. Lunn died at a tragically early age due to leukaemia. Callaghan won 2 full Scotland caps, six less than Cunningham who also enjoyed success at Preston North End. However, the most famous name to play for Crossgates Primrose was Jim Baxter. It may be a source of some unhappiness in the village that a statue of the Scotland legend is situated in nearby Hill of Beath rather than in Crossgates. Baxter was born in the neighbouring community but began his football career at Crossgates. From Humbug Park he went to Raith Rovers and thence to Glasgow Rangers.

The club website names Martin Feeney as the club's player with most appearances - 356 between 1950 and 1960.

GROUND
Humbug Park is named after an eponymous pit located close to the village. As mentioned above a team called Crossgates Thistle played there before World War One. However, the current Humbug Park site was first used in 1933 by Crossagates Primrose who had been formed seven years earlier.

Humbug Park is close to the centre of the village but then so is everything else in this very small place.

The ground is aligned North-South. Entrances are at the north-east corner. Most spectators opt for the east side although the winter sun can make viewing problematical. However, this is the side for the pies and refreshments. The only elevated standing is behind the south goal. You may also discover some hitherto unknown species amongst the long grass and vegetation of this end of the ground. There is a very small shelter in the south-east corner which is generally occupied by a few locals. The ground has what was once an impressive concrete perimeter wall but large gaps in it allow unrestricted access to the ground for those who choose not to pay.

The pitch is surrounded by a typical Scottish post and rail fence, neatly painted in the club colours of Primrose and Blue.

In the 1990s and early 2000s Cowdenbeath FC frequently used Humbug Park for their SFL Youth Division matches.

SUPPORT
Unfortunately the population of Crossgates demonstrate very little interest in their local football team. Home attendances are unlikely to exceed a few dozen and the total crowd will depend on the number of away supporters.

GETTING THERE
Crossgates is only three miles from Dunfermline. The nearest railway station is

actually Dunfermline St Margaret's, which was opened fairly recently to serve the large new hospital on the eastern edge of the town. However, to walk from there to Humbug Park would take at least 35-40 minutes and along rather busy roads as well. Bus numbers 15, 19, 30, 33 and 55 pass along Halbeath Road, just 100 metres south of Queen Margaret Station, and also go to Crossgates. Any bus indicating Ballingry, Cowdenbeath, Kirkcaldy or Glenrothes will do.

By road you should exit from the M90 at Junction 3 Halbeath, signposted Dunfermline. At the roundabout, controlled by traffic lights, take the A92 for Kirkcaldy, but keep in the right hand lane. After 500 metres, at the next roundabout, take the B925 into Crossgates. Turn right at the traffic lights and Humbug Park is 100 metres on the right.

There is ample parking in the village. Players and officials can park inside the ground although the risk of a smashed windscreen from a hefty clearance is worth considering.

PROGRAMMES
Crossgates issued programmes on a regular basis during 2005/6 but were not producing them in 2006/7.

WEBSITE
http://homepages.tesco.net/~s.c.mitchell/
The club website is updated with scores and basic information. There is an excellent section with team photos of previous Crossgates sides.

TEN YEAR LEAGUE RECORD

1996/7	Fife League	10th out of 15	26pts
1997/8	Fife League	11th out of 15	24pts
1998/9	Fife League	12th out of 16	29pts
1999/00	Fife League	9th out of 15	30pts
2000/1	Fife League	9th out of 15	37pts
2001/2	Fife League	8th out of 15	47pts
2002/3	Fife League	6th out of 12	29pts
2003/4	Fife League	7th out of 10	20pts
2004/5	Fife League	12th out of 12	11pts
2005/6	Fife League	11th out of 13	23pts

TOWN (Population 3400)
Crossgates appeared on Pont's map of Scotland in about 1600. It was close to the strategically important Fordell Castle. By then Crossgates was at the centre of a coal mining district and this remained the driving force behind the village until the 1960s. A coal-carrying waggonway – a forerunner of the railways – ran from the mines at Crossgates to St David's Harbour on the Firth of Forth. By the 1820s Crossgates was an important crossroads where the Dunfermline to Kirkcaldy route bisected the route north from Queensferry.

The railway came to Crossgates in 1846 with a station to the north of the village. Later, in 1909, the tramway from Dunfermline to Cowdenbeath passed through the village. Coal mines opened and closed as reserves were worked but Crossgates never had fewer than six operational pits until the start of a decline in the 1950s. The National Coal Board operated offices at Crossgates which were later taken over by British Coal. The Mines Rescue Service was based in the village.

At one time Crossgates was on the main road north from Queensferry to Perth. The construction of the M90 in the early 1970s removed long-distance through traffic from the village. There is little to see that is of any great interest. Amenities are restricted to two pubs, a chip shop, post office, newsagents and a few other small businesses. Extensive new housing developments are underway and more are planned given the village's proximity to the M90 and the potential for commuting to Edinburgh.

SCOTTISH JUNIOR CUP RECORD			
88/9	Rd 1	Bye	
	Rd 2 H	Bathgate Thistle	1-3
89/90	Rd 1	Bye	
	Rd 2 A	Kilbirnie Ladeside	2-4
90/1	Rd 1 H	Dunbar United	1-1
	Rep A	Dunbar United	1-3
91/2	Rd 1	Bye	
	Rd 2 A	Linlithgow Rose	2-4
92/3	Rd 1	Bye	
	Rd 2 H	Aberdeen Lads Club	6-2
	Rd 3 H	Petershill	2-2
	Rep A	Petershill	1-4
93/4	Rd 1	Bye	
	Rd 2 H	Brechin Vics	3-0
	Rd 3 H	Inverurie Loco Works	8-1
	Rd 4 A	Downfield	1-2
94/5	Rd 1 H	Cuminestown	9-0
	Rd 2 A	Dundonald Bluebell	2-5
95/6	Rd 1	Bye	
	Rd 2 A	Cruden Bay	2-3
96/7	Rd 1	Bye	
	Rd 2 H	Cruden Bay	1-1
	Rep A	Cruden Bay	2-0
	Rd 3 A	Annbank United	0-4
97/8	Rd 1	Bye	
	Rd 2 A	Port Glasgow Athletic	3-5
98/9	Rd 1	Bye	
	Rd 2 H	Blackburn United	1-1
	Rep A	Blackburn United	0-2
99/0	Rd 1	Bye	
	Rd 2 A	Troon	1-3
00/1	Rd 1 A	Fraserburgh United	1-1
	Rep H	Fraserburgh United	1-1
		4-3 on penalties	
	Rd 2 A	Arbroath SC	1-1
	Rep H	Arbroath SC	3-1
	Rd 3 H	Kilwinning Rangers	0-2
01/2	Rd 1 H	Wilson's XI	1-1
	Rep A	Wilson's XI	3-1
	Rd 2 A	Hermes	1-2
02/3	Rd 1	Bye	
	Rd 2 H	Hermes	0-2
03/4	Rd 1	Bye	
	Rd 2 A	Newtongrange Star	0-2
04/5	Rd 1 A	Maryhill	2-3
05/6	Rd 1	Bye	
	Rd 2 H	Kilsyth Rangers	1-4
06/7	Rd 1 H	Hurlford United	3-4

HONOURS	
Fife Cup	1947/8, 1955/6
Cowdenbeath Cup	1928/9
West Fife Cup	1947/8, 1957/8

Humbug Park covers a large area, easily big enough for two football pitches. TOP picture is taken from the 'far corner' looking towards the entrance to the ground. LOWER picture shows the pavilion. Refreshments are sold from a window to the right of the building and very good they are too.

Page 22

FORMER JUNIOR FOOTBALL VENUES IN THE FIFE AREA

Further information about some former grounds is provided in the various club entries in this book. Those detailed below do not fit in so well with the club sections for one reason or another.

Many clubs have come and gone over the years and there are a few 'lost' venues to visit. Starting in the west, beyond the Fife boundary, is Clackmannan who played in the Fife Junior league from the early 1960s until 1995. They played at King George V Park which is still in use for minor football. No trace remains of Chapelhill Park, the former home of the senior club from the town. Close by is the small town of Kincardine which was home to Tulliallan Thistle. Most recently they played at Burnside Park which is still a football pitch adjacent to the main road into the town from Alloa. Sadly the boundary fencing which had been built to make the ground suitable for junior status was removed in 2006 so there seems little chance of a revival for this particular club. Valleyfield Colliery played out their latter years at the unenclosed Bon Accord Park (Also known as Clansman Park) in Culross on the shores of the River Forth. The ground is still in use for minor football. This is also the case at Blairhall where Woodside Park is a similar unenclosed venue.

In the Dunfermline area it is possible to visit three former junior venues. The peripatetic Jubilee Athletic (now Rosyth FC) were based at Ballast Bank in Inverkeithing for many years. This pitch, surrounded by a broad track, is still extant on the east side of the town, adjacent to the harbour. Athletic also used the Pitreavie Stadium which is basically an athletics venue located just off the main road from Rosyth to Dunfermline. In the late 1970s a Junior side of some strength emerged in Halbeath, adjacent to Junction 3 of the M90. They did well in the Scottish Junior Cup and switched several games to Cowdenbeath's Central Park because of the anticipated attendances. Village Park in Halbeath is still used for minor football.

At the north end of Cowdenbeath High Street, behind the library, lies North End Park. This was once home to the senior club in the town but more recently to Jubilee Athletic. It is now used by Amateur teams.

Little remains of the former homes of Junior sides in Central Fife. For many years the Violet Filling Station was the only reminder of Lochgelly Violet but it is now closed. Bowhill Rovers ground is now simply a public park. The original ground of Glenrothes Juniors at Dovecot Park is in the Auchmuty precinct and is still used for football.

In Kirkcaldy it is possible to visit Windmill Park, one of the former homes of Kirkcaldy YM, but there is little to see. The other grounds in Kirkcaldy and Dysart have disappeared over the years. The Levenmouth area once had various junior sides but the only ground that remains in use is King George V Park in Leven, formerly home to Leven Juniors. It is a public park.

In North East Fife there was an attempt to establish a Junior side in Newport-on-Tay in the late 1970s. They played at the Waterstone Crook Sports Centre which still has a football pitch.

DUNDONALD BLUEBELL

Ground—Moorside Park, Dundonald
Ground Phone Number—
Postcode / GPS Location—KY5 0BZ

Club Colours— Royal Blue

Club Secretary 2006/7— Andrew Davidson, 01592 721135

Look at a map of Scotland for the town of Dundonald and you will find that it is in Ayrshire. That Dundonald has nothing to do with Dundonald Bluebell who play at Cardenden in Central Fife. Strictly speaking Dundonald is the name of a separate former mining community on the edge of Cardenden although to all intents and purposes the two merge into the same. This is one of these amorphous Fife areas with numerous small settlements combining into a bigger urban area – as well as the aforementioned two, this one also includes Auchterderran and Bowhill, meaning it is the ABCD town! Bowhill is well-known in Scottish football as the home town and last resting place of John Thomson, the Prince of Goalkeepers, killed while playing for Celtic against Rangers in 1931. His grave, in Bowhill Cemetery, is a place that all football supporters should visit at some point.

HISTORY

Dundonald Bluebell are the only Junior team still operating in the Cardenden area. In the past there were several others. Prominent amongst them were Bowhill Thistle (early 1900s) and Bowhill Rovers (1930-1951) who played at Wellsgreen Park. The Bluebell were formed in 1938 and became a prominent juvenile side around the time of World War Two and stepped up to junior level in 1946. They had won the Scottish Juvenile Cup in 1943/44 and 1944/45 and hoped to keep the team together for a further crack at honours in the junior game.

In their final season as a juvenile club they created a record by winning 3 Cup competitions in the space of 24 hours - on Friday evening, Saturday afternoon and again on Saturday evening!

The club's record victory was a 19-0 win over Valleyfield Colliery on 20th November 1951.

Honours have been few and far between for Dundonald. That having been said, like their neighbours Lochgelly Albert and Lochore Welfare, the Bluebell are great 'survivors'. They have enjoyed continuous membership of the Fife Juniors since immediately after World War Two when other teams have come and gone in that time. In the Scottish Junior Cup they have seldom progressed far. In the early and mid 1960s Round Four was reached on two occasions but the late 60s, 1970s and 1980s were a period of almost unremitting failure in the national competition. Reaching Round Five in 2001 was a new experience for the

Bluebell but by then the club was definitely on the 'up'. Ground improvements and hard work from a dedicated committee have seen the 'Bell challenge for local honours and in 2006/7 they were pushing hard for a place in the East Premier Division. They have hosted several Scottish League clubs in Friendlies at Moorside Park - most notably against Glasgow Rangers in 1993. In 2005 they also played host to a famous name from south of the border in the shape of Accrington Stanley - the visitors went on to win promotion to the Football League that season.

Bluebell have produced a stream of players for Scottish League clubs over the years. Most have gone to local Fife clubs but a few have gone further. The most notably is surely Cardenden-born Tommy Hutchison. Transferred from Bluebell to Alloa in 1965, Tommy went on to win 17 caps for Scotland during his long career with Coventry City, Manchester City and others.

GROUND
Moorside Park lives up to its name. Like Lochore and Lochgelly it has housing to one side and rural landscapes to the other. In Dundonald's case it is not unusual for spectators to be harassed by cattle leaning over the boundary fence, perhaps looking for a bite of their meat pie. Or perhaps not.

The entrances to Moorside Park are close to one corner of the ground. To the left, behind the goal, there is little more than a narrow walkway leading round to the far side of the field. On that side the grassy surrounds have a small covered enclosure to protect the spectators. The far end of the ground, behind the west goal, has some grassy banking. Most spectator facilities are on the 'pavilion side' where there are two covered enclosures as well as the pie and hot drinks facilities. An earlier pavilion burned down and was replaced with the present building in 1974. In recent years the club have undertaken significant ground improvements to improve spectator comforts. A new enclosure was built in front of the pavilion and two unusual covered areas created on opposite sides of the ground (see photo above for one of the 'Heath Robinson' style structures).

Bluebell have made their home at Moorside Park since their earliest days in Junior football. A 1947 vertical aerial photograph shows the ground in the process of being improved for the new season. More prominent on the photo is Wellsgreen Park, home of local rivals Bowhill Rovers. Their ground was located on what is presently Bowhill Recreation Ground and boasted a grandstand. Until their demise in 1951, Bowhill were Dundonald's closest geographic rivals.

SUPPORT
Compared to some of their neighbours Dundonald enjoy a reasonable support. The home support numbers around the hundred mark and some of them take the trouble to travel to away matches.

GETTING THERE
Cardenden railway station is close to the ground. Ten minutes walk up a steady hill brings you to Dundonald. Turn right into the housing scheme at the Post

Office, and then take first left. The ground is straight in front of you.

By car there are different options depending on which way you come. The main A92 Dunfermline to Kirkcaldy and Glenrothes road passes very close to the ground but there is no suitable exit. The easiest access is from the Cardenden / Kirkcaldy West exit. Head for Cardenden on the B981, pass beneath the railway and then take a sharp left (signposted for the station) after about 300 metres. Continue past the railway station and follow the directions above. The more adventurous may wish to try a cross country route from Junction 3 of the M90, via Crossgates, Cowdenbeath, Lumphinnans and Lochgelly but this I not for the faint hearted or the tardy.

Bus services 15 and 33 (Dunfermline to Kirkcaldy) and 35 (Kirkcaldy to Glenrothes) all visit Dundonald Turing Circle.

Regardless of how you arrive there is no sign of Moorside Park from the main road. The ground is to your right as you head out of Cardenden, behind the housing scheme known properly as Dundonald Park. If you reach open country and pass North Dundonald Farm you've gone too far!

PROGRAMMES
Dundonald are not noted for being regular programme issuers. The friendlies mentioned above against senior opposition - Glasgow Rangers and Accrington Stanley - did prompt them to issue but they have never done so on a regular basis.

WEBSITE
The club website can be found at: http://dundonaldbluebell.com/ This is one of the more attractive and best-maintained websites amongst the Fife clubs. It includes a section with old team photos dating back to the immediate post-war years.

TEN YEAR LEAGUE RECORD

1996/7	Fife League	4th out of 15	34pts
1997/8	Fife League	10th out of 15	24pts
1998/9	Fife League	8th out of 16	45pts
1999/00	Fife League	11th out of 15	29pts
2000/1	Fife League	8th out of 15	45pts
2001/2	Fife League	9th out of 15	45pts
2002/3	Fife League	3rd out of 12	41pts
2003/4	Fife League	3rd out of 10	33pts
2004/5	Fife League	9th out of 12	21pts
2005/6	Fife League	6th out of 13	34pts

TOWN (Population 5400, including Cardenden and Auchterderran)
The Dundonald Coal Company was in business by 1892 when it sank the Lady Helen shaft. However, their major work was the creation of the Dundonald Mine in 1895. It remained open until 1964 – it was well known for its Pipe Band. The Dundonald Park housing scheme, adjacent to Moorside Park, was created to replace sub-standard miners rows during the inter-war and

immediate post-war years. The wider settlement of Cardenden has spawned some famous names — as well as the aforementioned John Thomson, it was the home town of James Black (inventor of beta blockers) and of Ian Rankin (author of the Inspector Rebus series of novels). There is little to attract the casual visitor to the Cardenden-Dundonald-Bowhill-Auchterderran conglomeration. Local services are basic. There is a pub (Village Inn) on the main road close to Moorside Park which welcomes football supporters.

ABOVE—Little has changed at the east end between 1990 and 2007. BELOW But plenty has changed on the main side with the new enclosure sitting in front of the old pavilion.

SCOTTISH JUNIOR CUP RECORD

88/9	Rd 1	H	Bo'ness United	1-1
	Rep	A	Bo'ness United	1-5
89/90	Rd 1	A	Maybole	1-3
90/1	Rd 1	Bye		
	Rd 2	A	Troon	0-1
91/2	Rd 1	A	Benburb	1-2
92/3	Rd 1	Bye		
	Rd 2	A	Baillieston	0-1
93/4	Rd 1	Bye		
	Rd 2	A	Carluke Rovers	3-1
	Rd 3	A	Maryhill	3-3
	Rep	H	Maryhill	2-4
94/5	Rd 1	Bye		
	Rd 2	H	Crossgates Primrose	5-2
	Rd 3	H	Camelon	1-3
95/6	Rd 1	H	Bo'ness United	1-2
96/7	Rd 1	A	Glasgow Perthshire	1-2
97/8	Rd 1	Bye		
	Rd 2	A	Deveronside	4-0
	Rd 3	H	Fauldhouse United	2-1
	Rd 4	H	Arthurlie	1-4
98/9	Rd 1	A	Blackburn United	0-5
99/0	Rd 1	H	Cruden Bay	0-1
00/1	Rd 1	Bye		
	Rd 2	H	Tranent	2-2
	Rep	A	Tranent	4-0
	Rd 3	H	Blantyre Vics	3-2
	Rd 4	A	Stoneyburn	2-2
	Rep	H	Stoneyburn	1-0
	Rd 5	A	Renfrew	1-5
01/2	Rd 1	H	Longside	5-1
	Rd 2	H	Vale of Clyde	1-2
02/3	Rd 1	Bye		
	Rd 2	H	Rutherglen Glencairn	2-1
	Rd 3	A	Downfield	1-1
	Rep	H	Downfield	2-1
	Rd 4	A	Irvine Meadow	1-2
03/4	Rd 1	Bye		
	Rd 2	A	Larkhall Thistle	1-1
	Rep	H	Larkhall Thistle	0-3
04/5	Rd 1	H	Banks o' Dee	1-2
05/6	Rd 1	H	Beith	1-2
06/7	Rd 1	H	Fochabers	1-0
	Rd 2	A	Thornton Hibs	7-1
	Rd 3	A	Carnoustie Panmure	2-1
	Rd 4	A	Musselburgh Athletic	0-3

HONOURS

Fife County League	1951/2, 1956/7, 1957/8
Fife Regional League	1982/3
Fife Cup	1954/5, 1991/2
Cowdenbeath Cup	1964/5, 1969/70
Express Cup	1965/6
Laidlaw Shield	1991/2, 1992/3
Mitchell Cup	1947/8, 1948/9

GLENROTHES

Ground—Warout Stadium, Glenrothes
Ground Phone Number—01592 755067
Postcode / GPS Location—KY7 4JY

Club Colours— Red and White

Club Secretary 2006/7— Robert Adamson, 01592 759395

The Central Fife New Town of Glenrothes was formally established in 1948, although much of the development was undertaken during the 1960s and early 1970s. It was envisaged as a coal-mining centre and the area set-aside for the town covered a large swathe of land between the existing villages of Markinch, Coaltown of Balgonie, Thornton, Leslie and Kinglassie. This included some small villages which remain 'visible' within the New Town, notably Woodside which is just a few hundred yards from the Warout Stadium. Coal mining was an expensive and short-lived venture so by the 1970s the town had changed its focus towards electronics and light industry.

HISTORY
Glenrothes New Town's Dovecot Park was opened in May 1958 by Lord Clydesmuir. It was located next to what was then Woodside School – now called Auchmuty High School. The ground is still in use for amateur games. Glenrothes Junior FC was founded in 1964 and played home games at Dovecote Park. The ground was prone to waterlogging and games sometimes had to be moved – the only other suitable venue in the town at the time was the CISWO (Coal Industry Social Welfare Organisation) Ground. In 1967/8 the Glens hosted Shotts Bon Accord in an all-ticket Scottish Junior Cup tie which drew 5400 fans – looking at the layout of the ground fewer than half of them will have been able to see the match. In 1972 the club moved to the new Warout Sports Stadium where they have remained ever since.

Glenrothes FC's finest achievement was winning the Scottish Junior Cup in 1974/5. Arbroath Vics (Home 3-1), Dunipace (Home 4-1), St Rochs (Home 1-0), Cumbernauld (Home 2-0) and Baillieston (Home 1-1, Replay 1-0) were defeated on the way to a Semi Final against Ashfield at Brockville. The Glens won 3-0 to book a Hampden appearance. Their opponents in the Final were Rutherglen Glencairn. A single goal by Cunningham in the 77th minute proved decisive. It is worth noting that in that same season, 1974/5, the Scottish Amateur Cup was won by Star Hearts from the village of Star of Markinch, just three miles from Glenrothes.

Since those heady days Glenrothes have maintained their reputation as one of the foremost sides in Fife but they have not been able to maintain a national profile. They were one of the founder members of the East Super League and fought a rearguard action to keep their place for four years before being relegated. This meant they were one of the founder members of the East Premier Division as well - and the signs midway through 2006/7 were that they could be on course for a quick return to the Super League. They remained undefeated in League fixtures until mid March.

The club has always been relatively well financed. Their home ground at Warout Stadium includes a large social club and function hall which is well patronised by locals. The club also run various other fund-raising activities. This means they have been able to afford to sign ex-seniors and top-level junior players to maintain their status.

GROUND
Since 1972 Glenrothes have played at the Council-owned Warout Stadium, reported to have cost £150,000 to build. The Grandstand has seating for 730 and there is steep banking around most of the pitch. Unfortunately viewing angles are not great because of the presence of a running-track. The pitch here can also suffer from drainage problems and some games in the 70s and 80s had to be switched back to Dovecote Park because of this. The best crowd at Warout was an all-ticket 5600 for a Scottish Junior Cup tie against Cambuslang Rangers in 1973/4.

The main entrances are beside the grandstand for which no extra charge is made. The stand undoubtedly affords the best viewing position but on a nice day the banking around the ground is better for catching the rays. There is some stepped terracing beside the stand but most is simply grassed.

The precincts of the stadium actually enclose a huge area of land. It is fairly common, again usually in the better weather, for local kids to amuse themselves on the running track, and by trying to drown each other in the steeplechase pool or bury each other alive in the long-jump pit. Thankfully the javelins are kept locked up.

There is a very large social club behind the glass partition at the rear of the stand where home and away fans are made equally welcome. This club is the main source of income for Glenrothes JFC and is a popular venue at the weekends for the more mature citizens of the town. It's definitely more pints, babycham and karaoke than trendy nightclub.

SUPPORT
Considering the size of the town Glenrothes have a disappointing level of support. Around one hundred regulars attend home matches and about a quarter of them travel to away matches.

GETTING THERE
Getting to Glenrothes by train is easier said than done. The so-called Glenrothes station is in Thornton and requires a taxi or bus connection to reach most of Glenrothes. Markinch Station has a less frequent service than Thornton but is actually closer to most of Glenrothes. However, the Warout Stadium is awkwardly located half way between the two making rail travel difficult for prospective supporters. Neither rail station is really within walking distance of the ground.

Glenrothes Bus Station, located next to the shopping precinct, is much more handily located. As the crow flies it is only about 500 metres from the Warout Stadium although this would involve you in walking through the Warout Precinct, one of the more lively residential neighbourhoods in the town. Visitors might be best to exit the Bus Station with the Golden Acorn pub on their left and to head 'half right' into Woodside Road. After about 300 metres, turn right into Warout Road and the ground is about 400 metres on the left.

By car most people will approach Glenrothes on the A92. Approaching from the south you will arrive at a large roundabout where you take the fourth exit (1 o'clock approx) signposted for Woodside. Continue up this road for a few hundred metres and turn left into Woodside Road at the Woodside Inn (get the theme!). After a further four hundred metres turn left into Warout Road and the ground is on the left.

From the north enter Glenrothes and continue to the large roundabout where the A911 bisects the A92. Turn right, following signposts for Town Centre and Leslie. At the next roundabout turn left and then keep straight on at the roundabout after that into Woodside Road. Being a New Town, the planners were rather fond of roundabouts. Turn right at a more conventional t-junction into Woodside Road and the ground is 400 metres away on the left.

PROGRAMMES
The Glens issued a few 'one off' programmes for Cup ties back in the late 1960s and early 70s. Some of these were in the style of the East Fife programme of the time and were produced by the same printing company in Methil. For many years from the early 70s through to the 2000s Glenrothes was a programme desert. But early in 2006/7 they began to issue a basic but very welcome match programme on a regular basis.

WEBSITE
Glenrothes had a website at:
http://www.glenrothesjuniors.bravehost.com/
Unfortunately it is not updated on a regular basis although it is still accessible.

They also have a web presence at:
http://www.webteams.co.uk/Home.asp?team=glenrothes
This site is updated on a regular basis.

TEN YEAR LEAGUE RECORD
1996/7	Fife League	3rd out of 15	39pts	
1997/8	Fife League	5th out of 15	49pts	
1998/9	Fife League	3rd out of 16	63pts	
1999/00	Fife League	7th out of 15	47pts	
2000/1	Fife League	7th out of 15	49pts	
2001/2	Fife League	2nd out of 15	56pts	
2002/3	East Super League	8th out of 12	26pts	
2003/4	East Super League	8th out of 12	26pts	
2004/5	East Super League	4th out of 12	35pts	
2005/6	East Super League	10th out of 12	22pts	Relegated

SCOTTISH JUNIOR CUP RECORD

88/9	Rd 1	A	Dundee St Joseph's	2-0
	Rd 2	A	Livingston United	2-2
	Rep	H	Livingston United	1-1
	Rep	N	Livingston United	3-2
	Rd 3	H	Cambuslang Rangers	0-2
89/90	Rd 1	A	Lochore Welfare	2-0
	Rd 2	A	Dunipace	1-0
	Rd 3	A	Deveronside	2-0
	Rd 4	H	Petershill	0-0
	Rep	A	Petershill	0-1
90/1	Rd 1	Bye		
	Rd 2	H	Newtongrange Star	1-1
	Rep	A	Newtongrange Star	0-3
91/2	Rd 1	A	Shotts Bon Accord	1-2
92/3	Rd 1	Bye		
	Rd 2	A	Largs Thistle	1-3
93/4	Rd 1	H	Rosyth Rec	1-0
	Rd 2	A	Neilston	0-5
94/5	Rd 1	Bye		
	Rd 2	A	Crombie Sport	6-0
	Rd 3	H	Maryhill	3-2
	Rd 4	A	Carnoustie Panmure	3-4
95/6	Rd 1	H	Haddington Athletic	4-1
	Rd 2	H	Bathgate Thistle	0-0
	Rep	A	Bathgate Thistle	1-0
	Rd 3	H	West Calder United	5-0
	Rd 4	H	Scone Thistle	2-2
	Rep	A	Scone Thistle	1-2
	Rd 5	A	Auchinleck Talbot	0-0
	Rep	H	Auchinleck Talbot	1-1, 5-6 on pens
96/7	Rd 1	H	Maud	7-1
	Rd 2	A	Dundee Violet	1-0
	Rd 3	H	Port Glasgow Athletic	1-0
	Rd 4	A	Fauldhouse United	0-2
97/8	Rd 1	H	Pumpherston	1-0
	Rd 2	A	Greenock	2-2
	Rep	H	Greenock	2-1
	Rd 3	A	Kilwinning Rangers	1-4
98/9	Rd 1	A	Dunbar United	2-3
99/0	Rd 1	A	Elmwood	6-0
	Rd 2	A	Forres Thistle	5-0
	Rd 3	H	Auchinleck Talbot	2-1
	Rd 4	A	Glenafton Athletic	0-6
00/1	Rd 1	Bye		
	Rd 2	H	Thorniewood United	6-1
	Rd 3	A	Longside	0-1
01/2	Rd 1	Bye		
	Rd 2	H	Carluke Rovers	3-0
	Rd 3	A	Troon	2-2
	Rep	H	Troon	2-2, 5-4 on pens
	Rd 4	H	Glenafton Athletic	0-1
02/3	Rd 1	Bye		
	Rd 2	H	Blairgowrie	1-1
	Rep	A	Blairgowrie	0-1
03/4	Rd 1	Bye		
	Rd 2	H	East Kilbride Thistle	4-2
	Rd 3	A	St Andrews United	1-0
	Rd 4	H	Lochgelly Albert	6-1
	Rd 5	A	Glenafton Athletic	2-1
	QF	A	Sauchie	0-0
	Rep	H	Sauchie	3-2
	SF	N	Tayport	0-1
04/5	Rd 1	A	Sauchie	3-3
	Rep	H	Sauchie	0-2
05/6	Rd 1	A	Kelty Hearts	1-1
	Rep	H	Kelty Hearts	2-1
	Rd 2	A	Camelon	3-0
	Rd 3	H	Ardeer Thistle	3-0

	Rd 4	H	Montrose Roselea	1-0
	Rd 5	A	Irvine Meadow	2-3
06/7	Rd 1	Bye		
	Rd 2	H	Bellshill Athletic	2-2
	Rep	A	Bellshill Athletic	0-3

HONOURS

Scottish Junior Cup   1974/5
Fife County League   1965/6, 1966/7, 1967/8
Fife Regional League   1969/70, 1970/1, 1974/5, 1975/6, 1977/8, 1983/4, 1984/5
Fife Cup   1967/8, 1970/1, 1971/2, 1972/3, 1975/6, 1976/7, 1978/9, 1985/6, 1997/8, 1999/00, 2000/1, 2003/4
Fife and Lothians Cup   1971/2
Cowdenbeath Cup   1969/70, 1971/2, 1972/3, 1973/4, 1976/7, 1977/8, 1983/4
East Fife Cup   1966/7, 1970/1, 1971/2
Fife Dryborough Cup   1974/5, 1978/9, 1983/4, 1984/5
Kingdom Kegs Cup   1996/7, 1998/9, 2001/2, 2003/4, 2004/5
Laidlaw Shield   1981/2, 1982/3

Apart from the main stand the remainder of the Warout Stadium has only a few steps of terracing.

MEET THE GLENS—In the late 1960s the club produced a fantastic cartoon book to commemorate their achievements. As well as cartoons of all the players (including future First Minister Henry McLeish), and others featuring key moments from matches, the book had a large photo of the then team and committee. Originally priced at a hefty 7/-, this is now a very rare and sought-after publication.

TOWN (population 39000)
Glenrothes New Town was the most northerly of the many such settlements designated in the immediate post-war years. Coal was to be the main employer – the Rothes Mine was built to the south of the town on a massive scale, yet scarcely produced any coal due to flooding and geological problems. Glenrothes had to look quickly for other employers and became a centre for the electronics and light engineering industries.

The New Town was designed on the 'neighbourhood' plan. The neighbourhoods were named after existing farms or small villages. Warout is one of the original such neighbourhoods, close to the town centre. The Stadium was a much later addition to the New Town facilities.

In the 1970s Glenrothes became the headquarters of Fife Council, rather than the long-established towns of Dunfermline or Kirkcaldy. This gave the image of Glenrothes a much-needed boost. It does have a reasonable shopping centre next to the bus station and only ten minutes from the Warout Stadium. The Golden Acorn pub, at the bus station, is a JD Wetherspoon establishment which also boasts bed and breakfast accommodation.

Municipal stadia are few and far between in Scotland. Amongst the Juniors only Greenock Juniors and Port Glasgow who share the Ravenscraig Stadium in Greenock currently use a similar facility. Lewis United of Aberdeen have recently left the Chris Anderson Stadium whilst it undergoes a revamp. Grangemouth Stadium was once home to Grangemouth Rovers but they disappeared from the junior scene almost thirty years ago.

HILL OF BEATH HAWTHORN

Ground—Keir's Park, Hill of Beath
Ground Phone Number—
Postcode / GPS Location—KY4 8DT

Club Colours— Red and White

Club Secretary 2006/7— David Baillie, 01383 513423

The name Hill of Beath has been prominent in football since the turn of the century.

HISTORY
Hill of Beath Hearts were based at Keirs Park in the late 19th Century before they changed their name to Hearts of Beath. They started out as a Junior side but played in the Senior ranks from 1897 into the early part of the 20th Century. The seniors folded in 1907 but re-emerged as a junior side in 1912. The 1920s saw a spell in abeyance but they were back in the Fife League by the 1930s. However, the outbreak of World War Two put paid to the Hearts of Beath side for good. From then until 1982 the village saw only amateur football played on Keirs Park. Other local junior sides occasionally used the venue for Cup ties but it was only after 1982 that the village boasted its own junior team again. Hill of Beath Hawthorn were formed as an amateur club in 1975 and stepped up to junior level in 1982 and quickly became one of the leading sides, not just in Fife junior football, but in Scotland.

In 1989/90, just seven years after joining the juniors, Hill of Beath lifted the biggest prize open to them - the Scottish Junior Cup. Along the road to the final they defeated some of the perceived giants of the Junior game in the shape of Linlithgow Rose, Arthurlie and Auchinleck Talbot. In the Final, played at Kilmarnock's Rugby Park, they won 1-0 against Lesmahagow. The Fife side proved that this success was no 'flash in the pan' by reaching the Quarter Finals three times during the 1990s and another Semi Final in 2003/4.

At local level they became one of the dominant clubs within Fife lifting the League title on nine occasions between 1987 and 2005, as well as numerous local Cups. Four wins in the inter-regional Fife-Tayside Cup, and one in the Fife-Lothians competition, are testament to Hill of Beath's quality. They have a fierce local rivalry with Kelty Hearts and the parallels between the clubs are obvious. Both joined the Junior ranks as recently as the 1980s and between them they have dominated the Fife scene since then.

After qualifying for the initial East Super League and finishing second in the inaugural season it was a major surprise when they were relegated the following year. However, the Haws rebounded straight back by winning the Fife Championship and re-established themselves at the top level.

Since joining the junior grade several Hill of Beath players have been capped by Junior Scotland. Jimmy Wright, Brian Ritchie, Bobby Wilson, Rab Duncan, Billy

Spence, John Mitchell and Marc Graham have all been honoured in this way.

GROUND

Keir's Park is one of the best junior grounds in Fife, if not the whole of Scotland. It may be small and compact but in terms of spectator comfort this is ahead of the game. The original venue used by Hearts of Beath was about 50 yards east of the current pitch and is now covered by housing. The present layout of the ground dates from the early 1920s. The record crowd of 6500 was established for a Scottish Junior Cup tie between Lumphinnans Wanderers and Preston Athletic in October 1947. Hill of Beath have also drawn good crowds – their record is thought to be 1781 for a Scottish Junior Cup tie against Arthurlie in 1989/90.

One side of the pitch has a narrow covered enclosure running three-quarters the length of the field. Both ends are essentially paved flat standing and there is concrete terracing on the other side. Within the past year or so a new covered enclosure has been built here, deeper than the one on the other side, and adding to the already impressive ground. It's one of the few grounds where underfoot conditions for spectators are better than for the players! The ground is visible when driving into the village from the south, with the team name emblazoned on the back of the enclosure. Keir's Park is one of the few junior grounds with proper turnstiles. There are separate entrances on different sides of the ground making segregation possible for bigger Cup ties. A unique feature of the ground is a large wrought-iron sign commemorating the Scottish Junior Cup win of 1990. The ground boasts match-quality floodlights that would be the envy of some Third Division SFL sides but these are seldom, if ever, used.

SUPPORT

Hill of Beath can bank on home crowds of well into three figures. For major games that can figure increases to between 500 and 1000. The club have lost some core support due to the relative resurgence of Cowdenbeath FC. In the 1990s Hill of Beath could regularly attract better crowds than their senior neighbours, but not so nowadays.

GETTING THERE

Cowdenbeath railway station is the closest rail access to the ground although it is a couple of miles away. Walking from the station to Hill of Beath's ground would take the best part of half an hour. Leaving the station head south down High Street to the 'cross' at the Bruce Hotel. Turn right into Broad Street and keep going for almost a mile. Pass the bus garage on the right and eventually turn right into Woodend Place opposite the Silver Birch pub. Continue straight on to the end where you should turn left. Your are now in Hill of Beath and the football ground is on the right.

Bus services 15, 19, 30 and 33 all pass through Hill of Beath. All of these leave from Dunfermline with the 15 and 33 also serving Kirkcaldy. Numbers 15, 30 and 33 are fine for getting from Cowdenbeath Station to Hill of Beath.

By car, drivers are best to exit the M90 at Junction 3 Halbeath. Take the A92 for Kirkcaldy but remain in the right hand lane - after four hundred yards, at a second roundabout, take the Crossgates turning. In Crossgates village centre turn left at the traffic lights. In about half a mile Hill of Beath is signposted to the left. Keir's Park is visible on the left as you enter the village.

PROGRAMMES
Hill of Beath have been intermittent producers of programmes over the years. Scottish Junior Cup ties are probably the most likely games to see a programme issued but they have been known to produce them for other games as well.

WEBSITE
The Hill of Beath website is one of the better ones in the Juniors and can be found at:
http://www.hillofbeathhawthorn.freeserve.co.uk/

TEN YEAR LEAGUE RECORD

1996/7	Fife League	2nd out of 15	47pts	
1997/8	Fife League	1st out of 15	75pts	
1998/9	Fife League	2nd out of 16	76pts	
1999/00	Fife League	1st out of 15	69pts	
2000/1	Fife League	2nd out of 15	61pts	
2001/2	Fife League	2nd out of 15	69pts	
2002/3	East Super Leag	2nd out of 12	50pts	
2003/4	East Super Leag	11th out of 12	20pts	Relegated
2004/5	Fife League	1st out of 12	54pts	Promoted
2005/6	East Super Leag	3rd out of 12	38pts	

TOWN (Population 1000 approx)
Hill of Beath has long been a separate community from its immediate neighbours. Crossgates and Cowdenbeath may be better-known but Hill of Beath has its own history. Like everywhere else in the area it was a mining community. The present-day village is almost totally comprised of more modern houses that were built to replace the overcrowded miners rows between the 1930s and the 1950s. Possibly the only visitor attraction is a life-size statue of Jim Baxter which can be found just off the main road and close to the football ground. Wayward-genius Baxter was born in Hill of Beath although he never played for the local side. His early football was in the colours of closest neighbours Crossgates Primrose.

SCOTTISH JUNIOR CUP RECORD

88/9	Rd 1	Bye		
	Rd 2	A	Brechin Vics	2-1
	Rd 3	A	Oakley United	1-2
89/90	Rd 1	A	Inverurie Loco Works	1-0
	Rd 2	H	Lochgelly Albert	3-0
	Rd 3	H	Broxburn Athletic	1-0
	Rd 4	A	Forfar West End	0-0
	Rep	H	Forfar West End	5-0
	Rd 5	H	Auchinleck Talbot	3-0
	QF	A	Arthurlie	2-2
	Rep	H	Arthurlie	0-0
	Rep	N	Arthurlie	3-2
	SF	N	Linlithgow Rose	2-0
	F	N	Lesmahagow	1-0
90/1	Rd 1	Bye		
	Rd 2	A	Benburb	1-1
	Rep	H	Benburb	2-2
	Rep	N	Benburb	3-2
	Rd 3	H	Maryhill	1-1
	Rep	A	Maryhill	3-3
	Rep	N	Maryhill	2-3
91/2	Rd 1	Bye		
	Rd 2	H	Newtongrange Star	3-1
	Rd 3	H	Downfield	3-0
	Rd 4	A	Lanark United	1-0
	Rd 5	H	Arbroath SC	4-0
	QF	A	Auchinleck Talbot	0-0
	Rep	H	Auchinleck Talbot	0-5
92/3	Rd 1	Bye		
	Rd 2	A	Kilwinning Rangers	5-3
	Rd 3	H	Downfield	2-2
	Rep	A	Downfield	1-1
	Rep	N	Downfield	2-2, 1-4 on pens
93/4	Rd 1	A	Livingston United	1-0
	Rd 2	H	Baillieston	4-1
	Rd 3	A	Kirkintilloch Rob Roy	1-0
	Rd 4	A	Lesmahagow	0-1
94/5	Rd 1	Bye		
	Rd 2	H	Whitletts Vics	8-1
	Rd 3	H	Longside	7-2
	Rd 4	H	Blantyre Vics	2-1
	Rd 5	H	Shotts Bon Accord	2-1
	QF	H	Lochee United	0-1
95/6	Rd 1	Bye		
	Rd 2	H	Newburgh	2-1
	Rd 3	H	Arniston Rangers	1-1
	Rep	A	Arniston Rangers	3-2
	Rd 4	A	Vale of Leven	0-2
96/7	Rd 1	Bye		
	Rd 2	H	Thornton Hibs	3-0
	Rd 3	H	Montrose Roselea	3-0
	Rd 4	A	Annbank Athletic	0-4
	Rd 5	A	Arthurlie	1-2
97/8	Rd 1	Bye		
	Rd 2	A	Lochee United	3-3
	Rep	H	Lochee United	2-0
	Rd 3	A	Annbank United	3-2
	Rd 4	A	Carnoustie Panmure	0-0
	Rep	H	Carnoustie Panmure	3-0
	Rd 5	A	Kilbirnie Ladeside	1-1
	Rep	H	Kilbirnie Ladeside	3-0
	QF	A	Kilwinning Rangers	2-2
	Rep	H	Kilwinning Rangers	0-3
98/9	Rd 1	A	Edinburgh United	1-0
	Rd 2	A	Largs Thistle	1-0
	Rd 3	H	Stonehouse Violet	4-0
	Rd 4	A	Sunnybank	3-2
	Rd 5	A	Auchinleck Talbot	0-2
99/0	Rd 1	Bye		
	Rd 2	H	Armadale Thistle	4-1
	Rd 3	H	Newtongrange Star	2-2
	Rep	A	Newtongrange Star	0-1
00/1	Rd 1	Bye		
	Rd 2	H	Glenafton Athletic	3-0
	Rd 3	H	Newtongrange Star	0-3
01/2	Rd 1	Bye		
	Rd 2	H	Thorniewood United	1-1
	Rep	A	Thorniewood United	5-0
	Rd 3	H	Kirrie Thistle	4-3
	Rd 4	A	Bellshill Athletic	4-2
	Rd 5	A	Kilwinning Rangers	1-3
02/3	Rd 1	H	Forfar Albion	2-1
	Rd 2	A	Ashfield	2-1
	Rd 3	A	Shotts Bon Accord	2-0
	Rd 4	A	Petershill	0-0
	Rep	H	Petershill	0-3
03/4	Rd 1	Bye		
	Rd 2	A	Blairgowrie	4-2
	Rd 3	A	Larkhall Thistle	1-1
	Rep	H	Larkhall Thistle	1-1, 5-4 on pens
	Rd 4	H	Culter	2-0
	Rd 5	H	Linlithgow Rose	4-1
	QF	A	Musselburgh Athletic	0-0
	Rep	H	Musselburgh Athletic	2-1
	SF	N	Carnoustie Panmure	3-4
04/5	Rd 1	Bye		
	Rd 2	H	St Rochs	2-0
	Rd 3	H	Wishaw	0-0
	Rep	A	Wishaw	3-3, 5-3 on pens
	Rd 4	H	Blackburn United	3-1
	Rd 5	A	Pollok	2-3
05/6	Rd 1	H	Camelon	0-3

HONOURS
Scottish Junior Cup 1989/90
Fife Regional League 1986/7, 1988/9, 1993/4, 1994/5, 1995/6, 1997/8, 1999/2000, 2001/2, 2004/5
Fife and Lothians Cup 1995/6
Fife-Tayside Cup 1995/6, 2000/1, 2001/2, 2002/3
Fife Cup 1990/1, 1993/4, 1994/5, 1995/6, 2001/2, 2002/3
Cowdenbeath Cup 1988/9, 1989/90, 1991/2, 1993/4, 1994/5, 1996/7, 1997/8, 2000/1, 2002/3
East Coast Windows Cup 1990/1
Fife Dryborough Cup 1985/6
Kingdom Kegs Cup 1997/8, 1999/2000
Laidlaw Shield 1985/6, 1987/8, 1989/90
Redwood Leisure Cup 2004/5
Fife League Cup 2004/5
Peddie Smith Maloco Cup 2005/6

The Haws are not shy about broadcasting their name to the community and neither should they be. Since joining the Junior grade in the 1980s they have been one of the most consistent sides in Scotland, and boast one of the best junior grounds in the country.

Known first as the Crieff Road Stadium and then as Simpson Park, the home of Jeanfield Swifts, was demolished in late 2006. The excellent pavilion, which was the envy of many other clubs in the area, was on the northeast side of the ground. Opposite was a small covered enclosure. By the time this picture was taken it was shorn of its roofing and was daubed with graffiti from the local youth. By Spring 2007 new houses were being built on the site and no trace of Perth's one-time foremost non-league venue remained. With Muirton Park also razed to the ground this part of Perth has lost two excellent grounds.

JEANFIELD SWIFTS

Ground— Bute Drive, North Muirton, Perth
Ground Phone Number—
Postcode / GPS Location— PH1 3BG

Club Colours— Black and White

Club Secretary 2006/7— Iain Armit, 01738 633310

HISTORY

Jeanfield Swifts were formed in 1928/9 when Hamish Methven and Ian McLeish banded together boys from the Jeanfield district of Perth to play against other districts of the town. They moved on to join the Perth City Boys League for two seasons before moving up to the Perthshire Juvenile League. The first club secretary / treasurer was Willie Simpson who served Swifts for 25 years. Swifts first made application to join the Perth Junior League ranks in 1936 but their attempt was defeated. The reason given was that the Juniors did not want to be seen as 'poaching' a club from the Juvenile ranks. Swifts were as well organised and better-financed than most Junior cubs and they applied again in 1938. This time they were refused with various Junior officials coming up with assorted reasons for the knock-back. Swifts were the only Juvenile club in Perth and some clubs were concerned that their supply of players would be threatened in Swifts stepped up. Others stated that the Junior league was already big enough. The Junior League did say that Swifts, and fellow applicants Ruthvenvale, would be considered if a vacancy arose. Perversely the Perthshire Junior Football Association, but not the league, did grant entry to Jeanfield Swifts and to Ruthvenvale – this meant they could play in Junior Cups but had no League membership!

Swifts Secretary Willie Simpson appealed to the Scottish Junior FA who remitted the decision back to the Perthshire Junior League for further consideration. An EGM of the League was held in early August, on the eve of the 1938/9 season, and this time Swifts were admitted. Many of their players had signed for other clubs thinking that Swifts were to be confined to the Juveniles.

By September 3rd Swifts had put together a side and played their first Junior game against Roselea at the Recreation Grounds. Roselea won 3-2. The following week they played Blairgowrie United at Davie Park in the Scottish Junior Cup, losing 4-2. It took until September 24th for Swifts to win a Junior game and they did so in style – defeating St Leonards 8-1.

In June 1949 the club applied to Perth Town Council to be granted a piece of land so that they could develop their own ground. In 1950 the plans for a new ground just off the Crieff Road were approved. Swifts hoped that having their own ground, rather than playing on the Inch with many other clubs, would increase their income. The ground would also be used for local Cup Finals and representative games.

The Crieff Road ground was opened o 12th August 1952 with a game against Newburgh. Swifts won 2-1. The club actually left the park for a year or so in the 50s to allow for further improvements but were back in time for the 1958/9 season. The name of the ground was changed to Simpson Park in 1963 - St Johnstone played a special game against Swifts to mark the occasion.

Through time a large Social Club was built at the ground and for a spell it was a valuable money earner for the club. The time for such clubs came and went and it eventually closed.

From around 2000 Swifts were known to be considering a move away from Simpson Park. The ground was too big for their needs and it was also a prime piece of real estate in prosperous Perth. In 2006 they moved to a new site at North Muirton and by early 2007 Simpson Park and its facilities had been bulldozed to oblivion.

On the field of play Swifts have known good times and bad. Within the restricted confines of Perthshire Junior football they were habitually one of the top sides. When the Perthshire clubs went in with the Dundee and Angus sides in 1968 Swifts found things more difficult and the trophies came less frequently. The rise of Kinnoull in the 1980s saw Swifts eclipsed as the foremost Junior side in the town although don't tell that to their hard core of loyal supporters!

Swifts are now registered as a Community Amateur Sports Club. This has certain tax advantages and any club could become a CASC if they can satisfy the following criteria: Is membership of the club open to the whole community? Are all the club's facilities available to members without discrimination? Does the club's constitution prevent profits of the club being distributed amongst its members (i.e. any profits must go back into the club)? Does the club provide facilities for & encourage participation in eligible sports? Does the club's constitution provide that on dissolution of the club, any net assets are to be applied for approved sporting or charitable purposes?

GROUND
In October 2006 Jeanfield Swifts left their home at Simpson Park and moved to the less salubrious surroundings of their new ground in North Muirton. Basically the ground has no facilities whatsoever other than a metal railing around the field of play. In January 2007 even the perimeter fencing was made up of temporary fencing sections. The changing rooms and other accommodation was within temporary modular containers.

For spectators all viewing areas are flat standing grass. There is no protection from the elements at all. In comparison to Simpson Park, which was full of character and had ample covered accommodation, the new Bute Drive ground is a big come down. Hopefully time will bring with it the addition of more spectator facilities and perhaps the locals from North Muirton will come to take an interest in the team.

SUPPORT
Swifts have a hard core of around fifty supporters who attend home matches. It will be interesting to see if they continue to support the club following the move

to such a poorly appointed ground. The local population of North Muirton have, so far, shown no inclination to go along and support the club. Even if they did they would not need to pay for admission to get an excellent view of the game.

PROGRAMMES
For a spell in the 1980s and early 1990s programmes were a regular feature at Simpson Park. They do not appear to have been produced for quite some time now.

WEBSITE
Swifts have a web presence at:
http://eteamz.active.com/jeanfieldswifts/
although it is not a full-updated club site. A more comprehensive website at:
http://www.jeanfieldswifts.co.uk
was discontinued midway through 2006/7, with a note that 'the committee wanted the site deleted'.

TEN YEAR LEAGUE RECORD
1996/7	Tayside League Div One	10th out of 14	26pts	
1997/8	Tayside League Div One	12th out of 14	21pts	Relegated
1998/9	Tayside League First Div	3rd out of 12	42pts	
1999/00	Tayside League First Div	1st out of 12	52pts	Promoted
2000/1	Tayside Premier Div	12th out of 12	9pts	Relegated
2001/2	Tayside League First Div	3rd out of 12	40pts	
2002/3	Tayside League First Div	8th out of 10	16pts	
2003/4	Tayside League First Div	5th out of 10	28pts	
2004/5	Tayside League First Div	6th out of 10	24pts	
2005/6	Tayside League First Div	1st out of 9	38pts	*

* No promotion due to league reconstruction

TOWN
Perth is a place that has plenty to occupy the visitor. Whether your interests are historical, cultural, retail, bacchanalian or gastronomic, there will be plenty to please you here. There are lots of places to stay should you wish to make Perth a centre for a holiday. The area close to the ground is possibly the least enticing part of town. It features a dull 'motor mile' of car showrooms, the depressed North Muirton housing scheme, and an Asda supermarket plonked on the site of St Johnstone's old ground. All the attractions are a mile and a half away in the town centre.

GETTING THERE
Swifts new ground is in the North Muirton area of the town – a 1960s council scheme which used to be prone to flooding from the adjacent River Tay. The ground is actually close to the former St Johnstone ground at Muirton Park.

Perth is something of a nightmare for car travellers with a series of ill-positioned exits from the main routes that pass the town. Coming from the south, be it by the M90 from Edinburgh or the A9 from Glasgow and Stirling, follow the Inverness signs. This will take you past St Johnstone's present ground at McDiarmid Park. At the end of the Perth by-pass (the roundabout after McDiarmid Park), turn right back in towards town. Pass beneath the

SCOTTISH JUNIOR CUP RECORD

88/9	Rd 1	Bye		
	Rd 2	H	Buckie Rovers	8-0
	Rd 3	A	Cumnock	0-1
89/90	Rd 1	Bye		
	Rd 2	H	Sauchie	2-1
	Rd 3	H	Downfield	2-2
	Rep	A	Downfield	1-1
	Rep	H	Downfield	3-4
90/1	Rd 1	Bye		
	Rd 2	A	Greenock	2-0
	Rd 3	A	Baillieston	1-1
	Rep	H	Baillieston	0-2
91/2	Rd 1	Bye		
	Rd 2	A	Formartine United	2-1
	Rd 3	A	Lanark United	0-0
	Rep	H	Lanark United	0-0
	Rep	H	Lanark United	2-3
92/3	Rd 1	Bye		
	Rd 2	A	Auchinleck Talbot	1-4
93/4	Rd 1	Bye		
	Rd 2	A	Oakley United	1-3
94/5	Rd 1	Bye		
	Rd 2	H	Stoneyburn	1-3
95/6	Rd 1	A	Bonnyrigg Rose	2-2
	Rep	H	Bonnyrigg Rose	0-3
96/7	Rd 1	A	Fraserburgh United	2-2
	Rep	H	Fraserburgh United	1-0
	Rd 2	A	Fochabers	6-1
	Rd 3	A	Whitburn	3-6
97/8	Rd 1	Bye		
	Rd 2	A	Royal Albert	3-1
	Rd 3	H	Beith	2-2
	Rep	A	Beith	1-6
98/9	Rd 1	H	Dyce	3-1
	Rd 2	A	Irvine Vics	1-1
	Rep	H	Irvine Vics	1-2
99/0	Rd 1	A	Oakley United	1-2
00/1	Rd 1	H	Cambuslang Rangers	1-3
01/2	Rd 1	Bye		
	Rd 2	H	Muirkirk	2-1
	Rd 3	H	Glenafton Athletic	0-3
02/3	Rd 1	Bye		
	Rd 2	A	Lochee United	1-5
03/4	Rd 1	A	Parkvale	2-2
	Rep	H	Parkvale	4-3
	Rd 2	A	Yoker Athletic	1-2
04/5	Rd 1	Bye		
	Rd 2	H	Buchanhaven Hearts	3-2
	Rd 3	H	Port Glasgow Athletic	0-1
05/6	Rd 1	A	Carnoustie Panmure	0-2
06/7	Rd 1	Bye		
	Rd 2	H	Nairn St Ninians	4-1

railway bridge and then take the next left into Bute Drive. Follow this road round for half-a-mile and the ground is on the left. There is a small car park on the left next to a modern church building.

From the town centre take the Dunkeld Road, past the Asda supermarket on the site of Muirton Park and then turn right into Gowans Terrace. Then take a left into Bute Drive and the ground is 300 metres on the right.

Perth railway station is on the south side of the city centre. Exit the station and turn left into Leonard Street. Follow this street to South Street and then into South Methven Street. This becomes North Methven Street. Turn left at Atholl Place and then right into Barrack Street which becomes Dunkeld Road. The walk from station to Bute Drive will take the best part of 40 minutes.

Bus services 5, 6, 9 and 10 link the town centre to North Muirton with a very frequent service.

Bute Drive—few facilities, no atmosphere and few fans—but hopefully promised improvements will materialise soon

HONOURS
Tayside Regional League Division 1 1972/3

Tayside Regional League Division 2	1976/7, 1995/6, 1999/00
Tayside First Division	2005/6
Midland Junior League	1943/4, 1945/6, 1946/7
Perthshire Junior League	1941/2, 1947/8, 1948/9, 1963/4, 1965/6, 1966/7, 1967/8, 1968/9
Constitutional Cup	1942/3, 1943/4, 1944/5, 1945/6, 1949/50, 1963/4, 1966/7, 1967/8, 1968/9
Craig Stephen Cup	1975/6, 1976/7, 1978/9, 1981/2
Currie Cup	1940/1, 1943/4, 1944/5, 1947/8, 1948/9, 1950/1, 1966/7, 1987/8
Downfield SC Cup	2001/2
PA Cup	1940/1, 1941/2, 1942/3, 1944/5, 1945/6, 1946/7, 1947/8, 1966/7, 1968/9, 1970/1
Perthshire Junior Charity Cup	1940/1, 1941/2
Perthshire Junior Cup	1942/3, 1943/4, 1944/5, 1946/7, 1947/8, 1954/5, 1964/5, 1965/6, 1972/3
Perthshire Rosebowl	1948/9, 1949/50, 1958/9, 1959/60, 1961/2, 1966/7, 1967/8
Red House Hotel Cup	1987/8, 1995/6, 2004/5
St Johnstone YM Cup	1961/2, 1965/6, 1966/7
Tayside Dryborough Cup	1976/7
Tayside Regional League Cup	1968/9, 1984/5

FORMER JUNIOR FOOTBALL GROUNDS IN THE PERTH AREA

Pictured above is Market Park in Crieff. The West Perthshire town was home to junior side Crieff Earngrove until 1981 and Market Park was their home towards the end of that time. When the club dropped out of the juniors they said at the time it was just a temporary measure to 'regroup' but they have not returned. Market Park is easy to locate in the town and is the venue for the annual Crieff Highland Games.

In Perth itself two venues are of particular interest. 'The Bowl', or Jeanfield Recreation Ground as it is correctly known, was home to Jeanfield Swifts, Kinnoull and Perth Celtic at various times. The latter club were formed as a Junior side in 1889 but dropped out of Junior football on their Centenary in 1989. Pictured below, 'The Bowl' is a natural amphitheatre which is still used for minor football.

Elsewhere in Perth the South Inch was a hive of footballing activity and still is at weekends. From the early years of the 20th Century through to the 1950s the Inch frequently hosted three or four Junior games at the same time. Punters used to go along and drift from game to game depending on which was proving to be the most interesting. Club officials took a 'collection' by carrying a blanket around the touchlines because it was impossible to charge admission for games on the Inch.

To the north-east of Scone, on the road to Coupar Angus, is the village of Balbeggie. This small settlement had a junior side from the 1970s through until 1996. They were based at Redfield Farm which is on the right hand side of the main road midway between Scone and Balbeggie. A more isolated and rural venue it would be hard to imagine.

The major 'lost' venue of Perth is Jeanfield Swifts old ground at Simpson Park. Sadly there is now nothing to see of this former ground.

KELTY HEARTS

Ground— Central Park, Kelty
Ground Phone Number—
Postcode / GPS Location— KY4 0AG

Club Colours— Maroon and white

Club Secretary 2006/7— Adam Peden, 01383 514009

Kelty is another former mining community which has seen its heart ripped out with the demise of the coal industry. Little trace remains now of the industry that provided the lifeblood for the community until the 1960s. The town has boasted several junior cubs over the years. The most recent incarnation, Kelty Hearts, have been relatively successful. Their predecessors included Kelty Rangers (who played at Seefar Park), Kelty Our Boys (Flowers Park), Kelty North End and a later incarnation of Kelty Rangers (North End Park).

HISTORY
Kelty Hearts emerged from amateur football to join the Junior ranks in 1980. They had no connection with any of the previous junior sides to have played in the town. Neither had Central Park been used by any of these other Junior sides. Their manager at the time was a certain Jim Leishman who later made his name in management at senior level and was still General Manager of Dunfermline Athletic in 2007.

Kelty quickly enjoyed success in local Cup competitions but it was 1990/1 until they won the Fife Junior League. Since then they have vied with local rivals Hill of Beath Hawthorn for status as the top Junior side in the Kingdom. At national level Kelty reached the Final of the Scottish Junior Cup in 1998/9, losing to Kilwinning Rangers. They reached the Final again in 2006/7 and gained a measure of revenge by defeating Kilwinning 3-0 in the Semi Final. The match was played on artificial grass at Hamilton's New Douglas Park. This set up a tough Final against Linlithgow Rose, scheduled for June 2007. In the 1999 final they could not match the feat of local rivals The Haws who had won the Cup a few years previously. However, Kelty have improved their reputation as one of the foremost Junior sides with a series of consistent results and successes against sides from beyond the East region.

As well as Jim Leishman there have been a few other well-known names who have taken up the reigns at Central Park. Andy Harrow and Colin Harris are well-known as ex-Raith Rovers strikers; Craig Robertson went on to roles with Dunfermline and East Fife; Jim McArthur is an ex-goalkeeper and well-known football agent. In 2007 Steve Leighton was the man in charge and had built a fine young side. Kelty, like many junior sides, had moved away from signing seasoned ex-professionals in favour of a less experienced but more ambitious type of player.

Over the years the club have produced a good few players for the professional ranks. One of the most successful of these was Andy Tod, a long-time servant to

Dunfermline Athletic who had a well-earned Testimonial during the 2006/7 season.

GROUND
Not surprisingly Central Park is not far from 'The Cross', the throbbing hub of the metropolis that is downtown Kelty. The main entrance to the ground is behind the south goal. Behind that goal all is flat (wet and muddy) standing. To the west side there is some banking and terracing and a small covered enclosure. Adjacent to this a tiny grandstand although some punters prefer to use it as a standing area. This replaced an earlier structure which blew down in 1988. The far end has some gently sloping grass banking whilst the east side houses the pavilion and is essentially just a flat area. The best view is from the raised area diagonally opposite the entrances. As well as being able to appreciate the game this also provides a great panorama of Lochore Meadows and the Benarty Hills. For some games another entrance is used at the far end of the ground adjacent to the former North End Park, used most recently as a trotting track. Additionally, for bigger games some of the local neds may avail themselves of the free admission available though the local Primary School playground and then by jumping down the six foot drop onto the west side banking.

SUPPORT
The people of the small town of Kelty will turn out and support the club for major games. Several hundred travelled south to Lanark in 2006/7 for the Scottish Junior Cup Quarter Final and around five hundred were at the Semi Final against Kilwinning. Any Scottish Cup ties or other important local games will attract a home support of a hundred or two. Even the most mundane fixture should see the home support break the three figure barrier.

GETTING THERE
No railway in Kelty these days. The nearest railway station is at Cowdenbeath, about four miles away from Central Park. Cowdenbeath is on the Fife Circle and is served by trains from Edinburgh. From Cowdenbeath to Kelty the only solution is to travel by bus. Service Number 17 operates hourly between the towns until early evening, the Number 18 is also hourly and runs slightly later, while the Number 56 links Cowdenbeath and Perth, via Kelty - also on an hourly basis.

By road Kelty is easy to find. It is adjacent to Junction 4 of the M90 motorway. Head down the hill into Kelty and turn left at 'The Cross' into Main Street. Then take the second on the right which is Bath Street. Central Park is set back from the road after about 200 yards on the left.

PROGRAMMES
Kelty have never been very prolific producers of match programmes. Scottish Junior Cup ties will probably elicit an issue. In common with some other clubs they insist on producing programmes comprised entirely of block capitals. It means it takes a bit longer to read!

WEBSITE
Kelty have a good website at:
http://www.keltyheartsjfc.com/

TEN YEAR LEAGUE RECORD
1996/7	Fife League	1st out of 15	55pts	
1997/8	Fife League	2nd out of 15	69pts	
1998/9	Fife League	1st out of 16	81pts	
1999/00	Fife League	2nd out of 15	66pts	
2000/1	Fife League	4th out of 15	54pts	
2001/2	Fife League	6th out of 15	52pts	
2002/3	Fife League	1st out of 12	57pts	Promoted
2003/4	East Super League	10th out of 12	20pts	Relegated
2004/5	Fife League	3rd out of 12	49pts	
2005/6	Fife League	4th out of 13	47pts	Promoted

The covered 'shed' at Central Park is sparsely populated for a midweek match against Dundee North End during April 2007. The good weather encouraged the partisan crowd of approximately 150 to spread themselves out around the field.

TOWN (Population 5450)
The modern settlement of Kelty has outgrown its original location. Kelty Bridge, just to the north, is an older settlement, with Kelty itself starting to grow after the creation of the Inverkeithing to Kinross turnpike road in 1753. The modern town grew up in the middle of an intensely-mined area. The mining villages of Lassodie lay to the south-west and Blairadam to the north. The main Kelty mines, the Aitken and the Lindsay, were east of the town, between Kelty and Lochore, and close to the Perth to Queensferry railway.

Kelty was linked by tramway to Cowdenbeath and Dunfermline in 1910 but the line closed in 1931 due to subsidence. Kelty also lost its passenger rail service around the same time.

Kelty itself saw the miners rows replaced by more modern council housing from the 1930s through to the 1960s. Despite being at the centre of an area with a population of up to 8000 facilities and amenities were and still are very limited.

For the visitor one of the possible attractions might be the Kathellan Farm Shop adjacent to the motorway exit. It serves good meals, sells a huge range of delicatessen items and has a children's farm area which is reputed to be worth a visit. Of the pubs in the town the Lindsay Tavern is a long-term sponsor of the football club and therefore worthy of support.

SCOTTISH JUNIOR CUP RECORD

Season	Round	H/A	Opponent	Score
88/9	Rd 1	H	Lochore Welfare	3-1
	Rd 2	H	Bonnyrigg Rose	3-2
	Rd 3	A	Bathgate Thistle	1-0
	Rd 4	H	Oakley United	0-0
	Rep	A	Oakley United	1-0
	Rd 5	A	Baillieston	1-2
89/90	Rd 1	Bye		
	Rd 2	A	Linlithgow Rose	0-2
90/1	Rd 1	Bye		
	Rd 2	A	Forth Wanderers	0-1
91/2	Rd 1	Bye		
	Rd 2	H	Bo'ness United	3-4
92/3	Rd 1	H	Pumpherston	4-3
	Rd 2	H	Blantyre Vics	3-0
	Rd 3	A	Port Glasgow Athletic	1-2
93/4	Rd 1	Bye		
	Rd 2	H	Rutherglen Glencairn	1-4
94/5	Rd 1	Bye		
	Rd 2	A	Dunipace	2-2
	Rep	H	Dunipace	1-0
	Rd 3	A	Bonnyrigg Rose	3-2
	Rd 4	A	Arniston Rangers	3-3
	Rep	H	Arniston Rangers	3-2
	Rd 5	A	Arthurlie	0-0
	Rep	A	Arthurlie	0-4
95/6	Rd 1	Bye		
	Rd 2	A	Saltcoats Vics	1-1
	Rep	H	Saltcoats Vics	3-0
	Rd 3	A	Kilwinning Rangers	0-1
96/7	Rd 1	Bye		
	Rd 2	H	Bishopmill United	7-1
	Rd 3	H	Lanark United	2-0
	Rd 4	A	Sunnybank	1-3
97/8	Rd 1	Bye		
	Rd 2	H	Beith	1-4
98/9	Rd 1	A	Culter	4-0
	Rd 2	A	Glentanar	2-0
	Rd 3	H	Musselburgh Athletic	0-0
	Rep	A	Musselburgh Athletic	2-1
	Rd 4	A	Dunbar United	3-0
	Rd 5	A	Fauldhouse United	2-1
	QF	H	Montrose Roselea	7-1
	SF	N	Petershill	3-1
	F	N	Kilwinning Rangers	0-1
99/0	Rd 1	Bye		
	Rd 2	H	Beith	3-0
	Rd 3	H	Stonehouse Violet	2-0
	Rd 4	A	Cumnock	0-0
	Rep	H	Cumnock	1-2
00/1	Rd 1	Bye		
	Rd 2	A	Newburgh	4-2
	Rd 3	H	Renfrew	2-2
	Rep	A	Renfrew	0-2
01/2	Rd 1	Bye		
	Rd 2	A	Sunnybank	1-1
	Rep	H	Sunnybank	1-1, 1-2 on pens
	Rd 3	H	Pumpherston	3-3
	Rep	A	Pumpherston	3-1
	Rd 4	H	Vale of Leven	1-1
	Rep	A	Vale of Leven	0-2
02/3	Rd 1	H	Glentanar	2-1
	Rd 2	A	Blantyre Victoria	2-1
	Rd 3	A	Stonehaven	2-0
	Rd 4	A	Bellshill Athletic	3-3
	Rep	H	Bellshill Athletic	1-2
03/4	Rd 1	Bye		
	Rd 2	H	Camelon	2-0
	Rd 3	A	Royal Albert	1-1
	Rep	H	Royal Albert	0-1
04/5	Rd 1	Bye		
	Rd 2	A	Shettleston	6-3
	Rd 3	A	Pollok	0-3
05/6	Rd 1	H	Glenrothes	1-1
	Rep	A	Glenrothes	1-2
06/7	Rd 1	A	Maybole	2-0
	Rd 2	H	Burghead Thistle	14-0
	Rd 3	H	Whitburn	1-1
	Rep	A	Whitburn	3-2
	Rd 4	A	Broughty Athletic	6-2
	Rd 5	H	Kilsyth Rangers	2-1
	QF	A	Lanark United	1-0
	SF	N	Kilwinning Rangers	3-0
	F	N	Linlithgow Rose	

HONOURS

Fife-Tayside Cup 1 997/8
East Region Fife District League 2002/3
Fife Regional League 1990/1, 1991/2, 1992/3, 1996/7, 1998/9
Fife Cup 1982/3, 1983/4, 1984/5, 1986/7, 1992/3
Cowdenbeath Cup 1981/2, 1984/5, 1985/6, 1986/7, 1992/3, 1999/2000
Fife Dryborough Cup 1981/2
Laidlaw Shield 1983/4, 1984/5, 1986/7

Kelty's Central Park is a most pleasant place to watch football on a sunny evening. Despite being formed as recently as 1975, and stepping up to the Juniors in 1980, Kelty have enjoyed great success.

KINNOULL

Ground— Tulloch Park, Perth
Ground Phone Number—
Postcode / GPS Location— PH1 2RW

Club Colours— Red and white

Club Secretary 2006/7— Graeme Chalmers, 01738 630326

HISTORY
The first Kinnoull Junior Football Club was formed in the early 1900s and folded in the 1930s. They have no connection with the present club other than the shared name. The present club dates back to 1943 when three Perth Academy boys - Ian McIntyre, Peter Moncreiff and Willie Mitchell - formed the club. They took the name from one of the 'houses' within the school - Kinnoull, although the name also applies to a district of Perth. Initially they played in the City Boys FA but in 1946 they decided to apply for membership of the Perthshire Junior League. They duly took their place in the League at the start of 1946/7 which was the first season of competition following the end of World War Two. Their first ever Junior game was on the evening of Friday 9th August 1946, away to long-defunct Auchterarder Primrose, resulting in a 1-1 draw.

The new combine had club rooms at various places over their early years. They started in the Cow Vennel in the centre of town before moving to two different locations in Bridgend. However, the biggest step forward came when local rivals Jeanfield Swifts moved from 'The Bowl' to their own park on the Crieff Road. Kinnoull took over the hut at 'The Bowl' (aka Jeanfield Recreation Ground) and gained home team playing rights for the council pitch there. For a while they had to share the facilities with another, now defunct, Junior side called Perth Celtic.

By the 1950s Kinnoull were a well-established junior side and around that time they provided several players who stepped up to senior level. Jeanfield Swifts remained the strongest Junior side in Perth but Kinnoull were rapidly emerging as their closest challengers.

In 1984 Kinnoull left the open spaces of the Jeanfield Recreation Ground to move into their new home at Tulloch Park. St Johnstone played a special friendly to open the ground. This coincided with an further improvement in playing quality and by the late 1980s Kinnoull and Jeanfield were comparable in size and standing.

By the mid 2000s it was Kinnoull who had forged ahead. They became the first Perth side to qualify for the East Super League by winning the Tayside Premier Division in 2006. Sadly by mid season it was clear that they were going to make a quick descent, but the creation of the East Premier League means that they will still be above their Fair City rivals in the league structure.

Kinnoull have made little significant impact at national level. They reached the Fourth Round of the Scottish Junior Cup in 1960/1 before losing to Inverurie Loco Works. The first three rounds were regionalised in those days and the Perth team had a comparatively easy run. They went one better in 1971/2 when they reached Round 5 (the last 16) before going down to Vale of Leven. In more recent times they have never managed to progress beyond Round Three.

Kinnoull have produced many players for the seniors over the years. Most have moved on to local clubs in the Perth, Dundee and Angus areas although a few have gone further. Derek Walker stepped up to Chesterfield in 1986 and became the first man to go from Kinnoull to an English club.

GROUND
The club moved to their own premise sat Tulloch Park in 1984. The ground is fully enclosed but has very little in the way of spectator facilities. The only entrances are from the main road (Tulloch Road) side behind the south goal. There is flat standing on all sides of the pitch and some areas, most notably the south end, are very boggy. Home supporters congregate on the west side and away fans head for the east side.

The pavilion stands in the corner of the ground and has a window from which the usual range of food and drink is sold.

The ground is entirely open to the elements and it is located in one of the less attractive areas of the town.

SUPPORT
Kinnoull have a thriving Social Club in the centre of Perth but few of their members make it to Tulloch Park for games. Home supports of fewer than one hundred are the norm. Having said that the club do have a hard core of real enthusiasts who have worked tremendously hard to raise the profile of the club and ensure that it is kept on a sound financial footing.

GETTING THERE
Tulloch Park lies to the north-west of Perth city centre, between the location of the old Simpson Park and St Johnstone's ground at McDiarmid Park.

Arriving by road the best way into Perth to reach the ground is from the A9 western by-pass. Take the exit signed for Crieff, but turn towards Perth at rather than Crieff at the top of the slip road. McDiarmid Park will be on your left as you drive towards Perth town centre. Tulloch Road leads off to the left after about three-quarters of a mile, just after you descend a hill. The turning is a sharp one and you almost double back on yourself. Tulloch Park is then a few hundred yards away on the right. Parking is available outside the ground. If your route brings you through Perth itself then simply follow the signs for Crieff until you cross the railway line on the edge of the city centre. The Tulloch Road junction is then about a couple of hundred yards on the right.

It is possible to walk to Tulloch Park from the railway station - it would take between 20 minutes and half an hour. From the front of the station turn left into Leonard Street and then sharp left again into Caledonian Road. Follow this road round crossing Glasgow Road and then turn left into Long Causeway. This passes a retail park and then crosses the main Perth to Inverness railway. Turn right into Feus Road and continue to the end. Turn left into Crieff Road, and then right into Tulloch Road to approach the ground.

Bus Services 1 and 2 from the city centre, but not the bus stance near the railway station, serve Tulloch Road.

PROGRAMMES
Kinnoull have been amongst the most regular and best programme producers in the junior ranks for many years now. Since moving to Tulloch Park they have produced programmes on a regular basis. During the 1980s these had a tremendous historical content. More recently the Noull News has been in more newsy style but with excellent coverage of the team, opposition and the junior scene as a whole. In 2006/7 Kinnoull's was arguably the best programme in junior football - not just in the local area but in the whole country.

WEBSITE
Likewise the website for Kinnoull is one of the brightest and best in the Junior world. It can be found at:

http://eteamz.active.com/kinnoulljuniorsfc/index

Unlike most Junior clubs Kinnoull also sell a limited range of souvenirs. Details are available through the website - don't rely on them being on sale at a match.

TEN YEAR LEAGUE RECORD

1996/7	Tayside League Div One	6th out of 14	31pts	
1997/8	Tayside League Div One	14th out of 14	3pts	Relegated
1998/9	Tayside First Division	8th out of 12	31pts	
1999/0	Tayside First Division	5th out of 12	40pts	
2000/1	Tayside First Division	5th out of 12	35pts	
2001/2	Tayside First Division	8th out of 12	28pts	
2002/3	Tayside First Division	2nd out of 10	42pts	Promoted
2003/4	Tayside Premier Div	5th out of 11	31pts	
2004/5	Tayside Premier Div	8th out of 11	24pts	
2005/6	Tayside Premier Div	1st out of 10	43pts	Promoted

TOWN
See the Jeanfield Swifts entry for more information about Perth. Swifts old ground, Simpson Park, lay four hundred yards towards the town from Tulloch Park. It was on the Crieff Road, adjacent to the railway line, on the town side of the tracks. Jeanfield Recreation Ground is also close by - from Tulloch Road head to Crieff Road, turn left and then right into Feus Road. At the end turn right into Jeanfield Road and the ground, or park as it really is, will be found behind houses on the right after a couple of hundred yards. This area is also known as Goodlyburn and has been used for football since the Victorian era.

SCOTTISH JUNIOR CUP RECORD
88/9 Rd 1 Bye
     Rd 2 A   Bon Accord   1-4
89/90 Rd 1 H   Craigmark Burntonians   1-1
     Rep A   Craigmark Burntonian   2-1
     Rd 2 H   Edinburgh United   0-1
90/1 Rd 1 Bye
     Rd 2 H   Lochgelly Albert   2-2
     Rep A   Lochgelly Albert   1-3
91/2 Rd 1 Bye
     Rd 2 H   Brechin Vics   4-0
     Rd 3 A   Johnstone Burgh   1-2
92/3 Rd 1 Bye
     Rd 2 A   Cuminestown   5-0
     Rd 3 A   Bellshill Athletic   1-2
93/4 Rd 1 Bye
     Rd 2 H   Broughty Athletic   0-1
94/5 Rd 1 Bye
     Rd 2 H   Newtongrange Star   1-1
     Rep A   Newtongrange Star   2-1
     Rd 3 H   Lewis United   2-2
     Rep A   Lewis United   2-2,
                                       2-4 on pens
95/6 Rd 1 Bye
     Rd 2 H   Pollok   1-2
96/7 Rd 1 Bye
     Rd 2 H   St Anthonys   2-1
     Rd 3 A   Cambuslang Rangers   1-1
     Rep H   Cambuslang Rangers   1-2
97/8 Rd 1 Bye
     Rd 2 A   Harthill Royal   1-3
98/9 Rd 1 Bye
     Rd 2 H   St Andrew's United   0-1
99/0 Rd 1 Bye
     Rd 2 H   RAF Lossiemouth   7-3
     Rd 3 A   Kilbirnie Ladeside   2-4
00/1 Rd 1 H   Nairn St Ninian   1-1
     Rep A   Nairn St Ninian   2-0
     Rd 2 H   Linlithgow Rose   0-8
01/2 Bye
     Rd 2 H   Bo'ness United   0-2
02/3 Rd 1 Bye
     Rd 2 H   Kirkintilloch Rob Roy   2-5
03/4 Rd 1 A   Auchinleck Talbot   1-5
04/5 Rd 1 Bye
     Rd 2 A   Stonehaven   2-1
     Rd 3 A   Thorniewood United   1-1
     Rep H   Thorniewood United   1-2
05/6 Rd 1 Bye
     Rd 2 H   Fauldhouse United   3-3
     Rep A   Fauldhouse United   3-3,
                                       2-4 on pens

HONOURS
Tayside Regional League Division 1 1982/3, 1983/4
Tayside Regional League Division 2 1980/1, 1988/9
Tayside Premier Division   2005/6
Constitutional Cup   1965/6
Craig Stephen Cup   1983/4
Currie Cup   1928/9, 1969/70, 1984/5
Herschell Trophy 1982/3
PA Cup   1959/60, 1960/1, 1961/2, 1967/8,
1969/70
Perthshire Junior Charity Cup   1928/9, 1931/2
Perthshire Junior Cup   1970/1
Perthshire Rosebowl   1957/8, 1960/1
Red House Hotel Cup   2001/2
Tayside Dryborough Cup   1984/5
Tayside Regional League Cup 1976/7

Kinnoull FC are rightly proud of their facilities at Tulloch Park. which was opened in 1984. The pavilion is spacious and well-appointed. Spectator facilities at the ground are very limited but with crowds of around a hundred this is hardly surprising.

Kinnoull have been prolific programme producers since moving to Tulloch Park in 1984. The clubs who do issue regularly, including Kinnoull, usually give great value for money in their comprehensive match programmes.

Page 50

KIRKCALDY YM

Ground— Denfield Park, Kirkcaldy
Ground Phone Number—
Postcode / GPS Location— KY1 2ER

Club Colours—

Club Secretary 2006/7— James Douglas, 01592 649759

Kirkcaldy is the biggest town in Fife and in football terms is best-known for senior club Raith Rovers. Several junior teams have sprung from the 'Lang Toon' over the years but without great success. Nairn Thistle (named after the Nairns Linoleum company) and Rosslyn Juniors both existed as recently as the 1950s. Currently it is Kirkcaldy YM who provide the Junior fix for football junkies in this part of the Kingdom.

HISTORY

The YM were originally a juvenile club. In 1970 they entered Junior football as a means of keeping their players together and offering them a chance to play at a higher level. Especially in the early years it was typical for players to come through the ranks from under age football to join the junior side although they did sign a few more experienced men to try and strengthen the side. Most notable amongst these was former Scotland Junior internationalist Ramsay Budd who came from Glenrothes, and was manager of the YM for a spell.

Kirkcaldy YM played at Smeaton Park from 1970 to 1973. The ground was well-developed and had a covered enclosure, having formerly been home to Nairn Thistle. Nairn had been the 'works team' of one of the big linoleum makers in the town and had played at junior level. By 1973 Nairns wanted the ground to expand their factory so the YM were forced to move to Coaltown of Wemyss where they groundshared at School Park with Frances Colliery. The Seaton Park site became the 2 Metre Cushionfloor Plant area of Nairns factory. In 1976 the YM moved to Windmill Park in Dysart – located very close to the former site of Station Park, where Rosslyn Juniors had played from 1910 until 1957. Windmill Park was not fully enclosed so the YM had to move Scottish Junior Cup ties to other grounds in the area – including Glenrothes, Dundonald, Leven and even Burntisland Shipyard.

Season 79/80 was memorable as the club won the B Division of the Fife League and recorded a fantastic 3-0 win over Petershill in Glasgow in the Scottish Junior Cup. Jimmy Murray scored a hat trick that day. The YM were beaten 4-1 by Arthurlie in the Third Round. Their league success remains the only honour the club have won in almost 40 years in Junior football.

In 2005 the YM reached the final of the Fife League Cup - their first local final. Hill of Beath defeated them 4-0 in front of a large crowd at Ballingry Rovers ground.

The club's best-ever Scottish Cup run was in 2005/6. This time they reached the Fifth Round before losing out to Petershill, who finally earned some revenge for the upset of all those years before. The YM's away win over Ayrshire side Glenafton Athletic in the previous round must rank as their best-ever result.

GROUND
Kirkcaldy YM moved to Denfield Park as recently as the 1990s after playing at other grounds in the town. These were little more than public playing fields whereas Denfield Park is fully enclosed. This means the YM can play Scottish Junior Cup ties on their own ground. Windmill Park, one of the YM's previous home venues, is only a few hundred yards from Denfield Park but doesn't really merit a detour unless wide-open playing fields without as much as a goalpost do it for you.

Ingress to Denfield Park is made though a gate at the south-west corner of the ground adjacent to the pavilion. There are no facilities for spectators at all - the field is surrounded by flat standing grass areas. The end next to the pavilion is very marshy so go along with suitable footwear! There is no shelter for spectators although trees along the northern side of the pitch can be helpful when the wind and rain comes from the appropriate direction.

Unusually for a junior ground there are no regular catering facilities within the ground. A van usually arrives at some point during the first half and parks outside the ground but that may be your lot. The best advice would be to take something with you.

The ground does allow the visitor to savour the unusual aroma that frequently envelops Kirkcaldy. A Scottish music hall song about a rail traveller included the line "Ah ken masel, by the queer-like smell, that the next stop's Kirkcaldy . . ." The smell in question is that of linoleum manufacture using linseed oil and the remaining linoleum plant is situated next to Denfield Park.

GETTING THERE
Denfield Park is not the easiest place to find – it is located in an industrial area of Kirkcaldy with only one road access. Travellers arriving by car should take the A92 from all directions to the Red House Roundabout – the more easterly of the exits for Kirkcaldy. From there take the A921 towards town. Take the second exit (straight on) at the next roundabout into Rosslyn Street which then becomes St Clair Street. Turn right into Junction Road and then half-right into Smeaton Road. Follow this street round to the left and just as you think you've taken a wrong turning Denfield Park will appear on the right. There is a small car park next to the ground but street parking is no problem. Nobody seems to live within a quarter mile of the ground.

Kirkcaldy's railway station is less than a mile from the ground although the walk is not very direct. Exit the station towards the town centre and turn left along Victoria Road. At Dunnikier Road, turn left and cross the railway. Turn right into Smeaton Gardens. Although the road is closed to vehicles follow the footpath through to Den Road. Denfield Park is on the left after a few hundred yards.

SCOTTISH JUNIOR CUP RECORD

88/9	Rd 1 A	Newburgh	3-3
	Rep H	Newburgh	3-1
	Rd 2 H	Turriff United	2-3
89/90	Rd 1 H	Ardrossan Winton Rov at Leven	0-3
90/1	Rd 1 H	Linlithgow Rose at Leven	0-8
93/4	Rd 1 Bye		
	Rd 2 H	Haddington Athletic	1-3
94/5	Rd 1 Bye		
	Rd 2 H	Turriff United	1-2
95/6	Rd 1 H	Fraserburgh United	3-3
	Rep A	Fraserburgh United	2-7
96/7	Rd 1 A	Blantyre Vics	0-1
97/8	Rd 1 Bye		
	Rd 2 H	Dyce	1-0
	Rd 3 H	Kirrie Thistle	0-5
98/9	Rd 1 H	Nairn St Ninian	1-3
99/0	Rd 1 Bye		
	Rd 2 H	Fauldhouse United	1-3
00/1	Rd 1 Bye		
	Rd 2 H	Bonnybridge	0-7
01/2	Rd 1 A	Kello Rovers	0-1
02/3	Rd 1 A	East Craigie	2-1
	Rd 2 H	Benburb	1-1
	Rep A	Benburb	2-3
03/4	Rd 1 A	Johnstone Burgh	1-2
04/5	Rd 1 H	Annbank United	1-2
05/6	Rd 1 Bye		
	Rd 2 H	Lewis United	1-0
	Rd 3 A	Wilsons XI	1-0
	Rd 4	Glenafton Athletic	1-0
	Rd 5 H	Petershill	0-1
06/7	Rd 1 Bye		
	Rd 2 H	Formartine United	2-1
	Rd 3 A	Camelon	0-2

HONOURS
Fife Regional League Division Two 1979/80

PROGRAMMES

For a while in the early and mid 2000s Kirkcaldy YM produced a full and detailed match programme which was often the highlight of a visit to Denfield Park. Sadly production of the programme ceased during 2005/6. The issue pictured below is one of their last, for a Scottish Junior Cup match against Lewis United from November 2005.

WEBSITE
None.

TEN YEAR LEAGUE RECORD

1996/7	Fife League	13th out of 15	15pts
1997/8	Fife League	12th out of 15	23pts
1998/9	Fife League	16th out of 16	6pts
1999/0	Fife League	14th out of 15	13pts
2000/1	Fife League	14th out of 15	7pts
2001/2	Fife League	15th out of 15	5pts
2002/3	Fife League	7th out of 12	29pts
2003/4	Fife League	5th out of 10	29pts
2004/5	Fife League	5th out of 12	33pts
2005/6	Fife League	5th out of 13	37pts

TOWN

Kirkcaldy, or the 'Lang Toon' as it is sometimes referred to, is a large town with 80,000 plus inhabitants. For a place of its size the town centre is not very exciting. The pedestrianised high street has little character and could be almost anywhere in the UK. One event which marks Kirkcaldy out is the annual Links Market. This is reputed to be the biggest street carnival / funfair in Europe with more than 200 fairground rides along the town's esplanade. It takes place every April and is popular with youngsters and the young-at-heart from around Fife. Unfortunately it is also popular with the local neds and ne'er-do-wells. For the rest of the year Kirkcaldy does not make much use of its extensive waterfront. It is separated from the town centre by a wide road which is frequented by the local boy-racers. Raith Rovers ground at Stark's Park, on the south western fringe of the town is worth a visit for its quirky corner grandstand. The stadium is a great example of what can be done in modernising an old ground without losing all its character and adapting plans to fit inconvenient spaces!

Page 53

LOCHGELLY ALBERT

Ground— Gardiners Park, Lochgelly
Ground Phone Number—
Postcode / GPS Location— KY5 9LL

Club Colours— Black and Yellow

Club Secretary 2006/7— Robert Beveridge, 01592 780221

Lochgelly Albert currently carry the mantle for football in this largish town. The story of football here has had many ups and downs but recently it has been a case of more downs than anything else. At one time, back in the 1920s, Lochgelly boasted Scottish League football but the local side were one of many to bite the dust as economic recession hit hard. Lochgelly went to the wall but neighbours Cowdenbeath survived and continue to thrive to this day. It is interesting to note that the teams that failed to survive those hard times were mainly from industrial areas – Bathgate, Broxburn, Dykehead, Bo'ness and the likes, whilst the teams from rural communities such as Forfar, Brechin and Montrose kept going.

HISTORY

The story of football in Lochgelly is very complex with senior and junior clubs forming and disbanding with confusing frequency during the late 19th and early 20th Century. Since the 1940s and the demise Lochgelly Violet, the Albert have been left as the main footballing representatives for the town.

The club have always played in gold and black - the same colours as Lochgelly United, the Senior club who represented the town in the Scottish Football League between 1914 and 1926. United's ground was at Recreation Park, close to the present-day centre of the town. Around that time there were two other senior clubs in the town - Lochgelly FC and Lochgelly Amateurs. Lochgelly United and Lochgelly FC existed side-by-side immediately prior to World War One; Lochgelly Amateurs took up the senior mantle when Lochgelly United went to the wall in 1927 but they struggled for support in competition with junior side Lochgelly Albert.

When Albert stepped up to the junior ranks in 1933 the town had been three years without a junior club. The previous team, Lochgelly Celtic, had gone defunct in 1930. Albert had actually been founded in 1926 and played Amateur football in the West Fife League until 1933. Albert were Champions of their league in 1930/1 and runners-up in 1931/2. By then the decision had been made to go up to the juniors and they sat out season 1932/3 to make the necessary preparations.

There are two theories as to how the club got the name 'Albert'. The first theory is that the club was named after Queen Victoria's husband, the Prince Albert. The people who believe this theory point to the fact that the clubs original team colours of Gold & Black are the same as the Royal Livery was at the time of

Prince Albert's death. However, the length of time between the Queen Consort's death and the setting up of the club in 1926 as an amateur club, makes this theory unlikely.

The second theory and probably the most respected, is that the club took it's name from a town on the River Somme. During the Great War of 1914-1918 many young men from Lochgelly not only fought, but perished, at the Somme. It is reported that most of the soldiers were at some time stationed in a town called Albert in northern France and a few not only played football before the war, but after hostilities had ceased set about founding a local team in Lochgelly. This may have been done to try and replace the local senior team Lochgelly United who had disbanded just before the outbreak of the war.

Albert's name is thought to derive from that French town close to the River Somme and commemorates those who enlisted, fought and died close to Albert.

The first junior game was away to Kirkford Juniors at Cowdenbeath's Beath View Park on 29/7/33. Lochgelly won 1-0. Within a couple of years of joining the juniors Albert were winning local trophies and had established themselves at this level.

Local rivalry was enhanced with the formation of Lochgelly Violet in 1935. They proved doughty opponents for Albert between then and 1949. At the end of 1948/9 the club went 'into abeyance' with a view to undertaking ground improvements - they never returned.

Albert's reputation as a formidable club was enhanced when they won the Fife and Lothians Cup in 1937 and were crowned Fife League champions the following year. Their halcyon years were immediately before and after World War Two with huge crowds watching games at Gardiners Park. Two Albert players went on to play for the full Scotland side after turning senior - Dave Duncan (East Fife and Raith Rovers) and George Aitken (East Fife and Sunderland).

Individual club records include Andy Harley's 96 goals during season 1935/6, and Jock Raeburn's total goal count of around 400 during the 1950s. In 1946 Albert defeated Nairn Thistle 16-0 in a League match.

The decline of coal mining and the pressures of tight finances saw Albert's fortunes decline in the 1970s and 80s. One surprise success came in 1974 when they won the National Dryborough Cup Final. Each region had a Dryborough Cup and the winners then played off for a national trophy—Albert defeated Petershill 3-1 after extra time in the Final played at Shettleston and picked up a £300 prize in the process. By the mid 1980s the club was on the point of folding but through the work of a few committed individuals they managed to carry on. During the late 1980s they had a tie-up with Raith Rovers to field the Kirkcaldy club's younger players.

Attendances in the immediate post-war years could be huge. The ground record of 11645 was established for a Scottish Junior Cup tie against Bo'ness United in March 1948.

Albert have provided many players to the seniors over the years. Ian Porterfield, scorer of Sunderland's goal in the 1973 FA Cup Final and later manager of Aberdeen and Chelsea is just one Gardiner's Park graduate, according to the club website. He certainly played for Lochore Welfare but may have been at Lochgelly before that. George Aitken of East Fife, Third Lanark and Sunderland is a certain product of Gardiner's Park.

Albert have never been past the Quarter Finals of the Scottish Junior Cup. They reached that stage in 1947/8 for the match against Bo'ness United which attracted the record crowd to the ground.

GROUND
Gardiner's Park is a truly awesome arena. Firstly, it is huge – if modern safety standards were not applied then this arena could comfortably house 10,000 spectators. They would be sliding about on steep grassy banks but it is clear that this ground was created to accommodate large numbers. Secondly, it must be one of the coldest and windiest locations in Scotland – the ground is on top of a hill and on anything but a warm Summer day it can be a chilly and exposed place to watch a game. Despite its size spectator facilities are virtually non-existent – hot refreshments from the side of the pavilion being as good as it gets

The ground has been inexistence since the early years of the 20th century. It was previously used by amateur and juvenile sides.

SUPPORT
Lochgelly do not attract much in the way of support considering the size of the town. The home support numbers a few dozen but they are lost within the huge slopes of Gardiner's Park. The lack of cover means there is no focal point for them to gather and any atmosphere would be whipped away by the winds that invariably batter the ground.

GETTING THERE
Lochgelly railway station could not be further from Gardiner's Park unless it was in another town. The station is on the north side of the town on the road out to Lochore and Ballingry; the football ground is on the southern fringe of the town, about a mile from the station and it's uphill all the way! Rom the station head uphill along Station Road, which then becomes Bank Street. Where it takes a sharp right turn go straight on, along Church Street. At the top turn right into Mid Street and then left into Well Road. Continue to The Avenue, turn left and then right to reach Gardiner's Park.

By road take the Lochgelly exit from the A92. At the first roundabout turn left. Keep going uphill into the housing estate. Gardiner's Park is on the left behind the houses - entry is up a lane after the houses. There is limited car parking space at the ground but the surface has more craters than the moon.

PROGRAMMES
Albert issued programmes for some games back in the early 1990s but do not appear to have done so on a regular basis since then. The programme pictured opposite was for a Scottish Junior Cup tie against Renfrew in season 2001/2.

SCOTTISH JUNIOR CUP RECORD				
88/9	Rd 1	A	Arbroath SC	2-2
	Rep	H	Arbroath SC	1-0
	Rd 2	A	Broxburn Athletic	1-4
89/90	Rd 1	Bye		
	Rd 2	A	Hill of Beath Hawthorn	0-3
90/1	Rd 1	Bye		
	Rd 2	A	Kinnoull	2-2
	Rep	H	Kinnoull	3-1
	Rd 3	H	Johnstone Burgh	0-1
91/2	Rd 1	Bye		
	Rd 2	H	Stoneyburn	2-6
92/3	Rd 1	H	Bon Accord	4-4
	Rep	A	Bon Accord	3-4
	Rd 2	H	RAF Kinloss	2-1
	Rd 3	H	Johnstone Burgh	0-3
93/4	Rd 1	H	Kirkintilloch Rob Roy	3-7
94/5	Rd 1	H	Buckie Rovers	2-0
	Rd 2	H	Strathspey Thistle	4-0
	Rd 3	A	Arniston Rangers	3-3
	Rep	H	Arniston Rangers	1-2
95/6	Rd 1	Bye		
	Rd 2	A	Tayport	0-6
96/7	Rd 1	A	Strathspey Thistle	2-1
	Rd 2	A	Lochee Harp	1-1
	Rep	H	Lochee Harp	3-4
97/8	Rd 1	A	Coupar Angus	2-5
98/9	Rd 1	Bye		
	Rd 2	H	Vale of Leven	1-1
	Rep	A	Vale of Leven	1-4
99/0	Rd 1	Bye		
	Rd 2	H	Islavale	2-6
00/1	Rd 1	H	Newburgh	1-3
01/2	Rd 1	Bye		
	Rd 2	A	Royal Albert	2-1
	Rd 3	A	Downfield	2-2
	Rep	H	Downfield	1-
1,			4-1 on pens	
	Rd 4	H	Renfrew	1-2
02/3	Rd 1	Bye		
	Rd 2	A	Banchory St Ternan	4-2
	Rd 3	A	Wishaw	1-1
	Rep	A	Wishaw	1-3
03/4	Rd 1	H	Strathspey Thistle	3-1
	Rd 2	H	New Elgin	6-2
	Rd 3	A	Glenrothes	1-6
04/5	Rd 1	A	Cumbernauld United	0-3
05/6	Rd 1	A	Forth Wanderers	1-2
06/7	Rd 1	A	Vale of Clyde	0-1

HONOURS
National Dryborough Cup   1973/4
Fife County League (West) 1937/8
Fife County League   1946/7, 1948/9, 1954/5
Fife Regional League   1973/4
Fife Cup   1934/5, 1940/1, 1953/4, 1956/7, 1957/8, 1977/8
Cowdenbeath Cup 1946/7, 1953/4, 1954/5, 1958/9
Express Cup   1959/60
Fife Dryborough Cup   1973/4, 1975/6
Mitchell Cup   1949/50, 1957/8
West Fife Cup   1934/5, 1936/7, 1955/6, 1956/7, 1971/2

WEBSITE
www.lochgellyalbert.co.uk
Pleasant on the eye but is not always updated very often.

TEN YEAR LEAGUE RECORD
1996/7	Fife League	9th out of 15	26pts
1997/8	Fife League	13th out of 15	22pts
1998/9	Fife League	11th out of 16	36pts
1999/0	Fife League	12th out of 15	26pts
2000/1	Fife League	12th out of 15	38pts
2001/2	Fife League	13th out of 15	14pts
2002/3	Fife League	11th out of 12	18pts
2003/4	Fife League	9th out of 10	17pts
2004/5	Fife League	7th out of 12	30pts
2005/6	Fife League	9th out of 13	26pts

TOWN
Lochgelly has often featured in the news for the wrong reasons. "The cheapest place in the UK to buy a house"; "The school with the poorest exam results in Scotland"; "Most deprived area in the country" - these are the sort of headlines that have been associated with Lochgelly. Actually, it isn't that bad at all. The main street is a bit tired and run-down but the same could be said of almost anywhere outwith the main cities these days. Lochgelly's problem is that it really isn't on the road to anywhere. There is no reason to pass through and precious little reason to go there at all.

O.V.D. Scottish Junior Cup
Season 2001- 2002
4th Round

Lochgelly Albert J.F.C.
V's
Renfrew J.F.C.
(Current Holders)

At Gardiners Park,
South St.,
Lochgelly.
Kick-off 2pm

75p

The pictures on the left were taken in 1990 when Gardiners Park was in a sorry state of dilapidation. By 2006 it had been spruced up and the scale of the banking behind the goal remains apparent. Spectators do not often venture onto this particular grassy knoll. A visit to Lochgelly Albert sums up what Junior fitba once was and what is has now become.

ABOVE—Village Park in Halbeath was a bleak and exposed venue on the edge of Dunfermline, close to the abortive Hyundai factory. The team enjoyed considerable success during their spell in the Juniors between 1976 and 1992.

LOCHORE WELFARE

Ground— Central Park, Crosshill
Ground Phone Number—
Postcode / GPS Location— KY5 8BJ

Club Colours— Black and White

Club Secretary 2006/7— David Moore, 01592 860343

Next door to Glencraig, home of Ballingry Rovers, lies Crosshill – home of Lochore Welfare FC. Lochore are one of the better-known and longer-established Fife Junior sides and they have produced many fine players over the years. The town, and the team, are pronounced by locals in the same way as the large city in Pakistan, Lahore. For those who have not perfected a Fife accent it is wise to stick to the more conventional pronunciation with the first syllable sounding like a stretch of inland water. English visitors must master the Scottish 'ch' if they are not to make a proper fool of themselves.

HISTORY

A team called Lochore Rangers competed in the Juniors in 1900. Lochore Welfare started as a Juvenile side and moved up to Junior level in 1935. They played at a ground known as Central Park, which was just south of another ground of the same name that had existed for some years. Just after World War One it was home to Lochore and Crosshill United – a short-lived Junior side playing in the Fife League. The new Lochore Welfare club had humble beginnings. Strips were obtained from defunct Amateur side Lochore Waverley and headquarters were established at the Burns Tavern in Crosshill. In 1936 the pitch was moved again – a further 50 yards to the south – to accommodate the development of a council housing scheme at Inchgall Avenue. The houses are those that adjoin the present Central Park. The last move necessitated the infill of a large hollow using rubble from demolished miners' rows.

By the late 1930s Welfare were enjoying considerable success in local competitions. This continued after the war and they are one of the few teams to have maintained continuous junior membership since those pre-war days. In 1947/8 James Cunningham scored a record 93 goals for the club – defences were obviously not on top in Fife Junior football at that time. In 1961/2 the club went through the whole league season undefeated. The 60s were a good period for Welfare with several local trophies finding their way to Central Park.

For a short spell in the late 1990s the club added the word 'Miners to their name, becoming Lochore Miners Welfare.

A number of top-name players started out at Lochore Welfare. Current Dundee United manager Craig Levein, ex Rangers, West Bromwich and Scotland winger Willie 'Bud' Johnston, former Hearts, Manchester City and Notts County defender Arthur Mann are just three of them. Lochore, along with

Lochgelly, also lay claim to Ian Porterfield, hero of Sunderland's 1973 Cup win, and by 2007 manager of the Armenian National Team. From Lochore to Armenia . . . globalisation or what? James Logie of Arsenal, Willie Gibson of Hearts, Willie Benvie of Raith Rovers . . . there are many great names that learned their footballing skills at Lochore.

In the late 1980s gangly teenager Gary Paterson was sold to Dundee in exchange for a set of tracksuits . . . he later returned to the club and as Player-Manager led them to their first Cup win in over 20 years in the Kingdom Kegs Cup Final of 2003 against Kelty Hearts.

GROUND
Central Park in Crosshill sits just off the main road through the town and is bordered by housing on one side and Lochore Meadows Country Park on the other. The Country Park was created in the 1970s and 80s by reclaiming a derelict mining landscape – Lochore was at the heart of the Fife coalfield. Pithead winding gear from one of the pits is preserved close to Lochore's ground.

The only entrances to Central Park are from the main road and take fans in to the corner of the ground. Once inside a steep rise takes the spectator up to pitch level. To the right, behind one goal, are the pavilion and changing rooms. This building was erected in the 1970s thanks to the efforts of the Supporters Club. 30,000 bricks were obtained from the demolished Nairn's Factory in Kirkcaldy and used to build the new pavilion. There are no social facilities for spectators other than the usual window dispensing pies, Bovril, tea etc. Straight ahead, down the south side of the pitch, is a small covered section. Viewing from this side, especially towards the far end, gives some elevation above the playing surface. The far end is basically overgrown flat standing with a poor view of the field. On the north side of the pitch the embankment is raised quite high above the field of play giving an excellent view.

Virtually all the spectator areas comprise long grass and bare earth so sturdy footwear is strongly recommended for any visit here.

The ground was opened in 1935 replacing an earlier enclosure where the pitch had been aligned at 90 degrees to the present. Building work necessitated the change in layout. The older ground had been home to a Junior side called Lochore and Crosshill United who played in the village up until the 1920s. Ground improvements were carried out in the 1950s with a new pavilion, covered enclosure and even the novelty of floodlights, although only for training purposes. The record crowd was set in 1964 when Johnstone Burgh visited for a Scottish Junior Cup tie.

SUPPORT
Lochore have a small but loyal support of around 50 die-hards. For bigger games more will turn out to support the team. To an extent there is also a group of 'floating' supporters in the area who will attend the most attractive-looking fixture at either Lochore, Ballingry, Lochgelly or possibly even Dundonald.

GETTING THERE
Central Park is only a few hundred metres further up the road from Ore Park so

the instructions for getting there are the same. The ground is on the same side of the main road as Ballingry's.

PROGRAMMES
Lochore produce a very good programme called 'The Welfare State'. It is certainly available for major Cup ties, and may also be on sale at other games.

WEBSITE
Lochore Welfare's website can be found at:
http://www.lochore.org.uk/index.html

TEN YEAR LEAGUE RECORD
1996/7	Fife League	15th out of 15	4pts
1997/8	Fife League	9th out of 15	33pts
1998/9	Fife League	7th out of 16	38pts
1999/00	Fife League	4th out of 15	53pts
2000/1	Fife League	3rd out of 15	60pts
2001/2	Fife League	5th out of 15	52pts
2002/3	Fife League	4th out of 12	38pts
2003/4	Fife League	6th out of 10	22pts
2004/5	Fife League	4th out of 12	34pts
2005/6	Fife League	12th out of 13	22pts

TOWN
Glencraig blends into Crosshill blends into Lochore blends into Ballingry in a two-mile splodge of urban development on the very edge of industrial Fife. This is the last outpost of the former mining communities – beyond Ballingry it is truly rural. Loch Leven and Kinrosshire are only a few miles away. Lochore and Crosshill have the usual pot-pourri of corner shops, pubs, hairdressers and the likes. The jewel in the crown for this area is Lochore Meadows Country Park. Created in the 1970s and 1980s, it converted a large area of coal-related wasteland into an attractive country park. It has a golf course, visitor centre, walks, a loch and even a beach! Central Park is adjacent to the main entry to the 'Meedies' as it is known - go and have a look. It really is hard to believe that this used to be slag heaps, burning bings, railway sidings, contaminated spoil and general dereliction.

Lochore's Central Park ground is now one of the tidiest in the league thanks to the hard work of the committee and volunteers. One of the more obscure matches to be played there was a pre-season friendly against Witton Albion in the early 1990s—the Witton programme noted how difficult it had been for their team to find Lochore!

SCOTTISH JUNIOR CUP RECORD			
88/9	Rd 1 A	Kelty Hearts	1-3
89/90	Rd 1 H	Glenrothes	0-2
90/1	Rd 1 Bye		
	Rd 2 H	Whitburn	1-4
91/2	Rd 1 A	Clackmannan	2-2
	Rep H	Clackmannan	0-
292/3	Rd 1 A	Livingston United	1-1
	Rep H	Livingston United	2-3
93/4	Rd 1 Bye		
	Rd 2 H	Vale of Leven	2-2
	Rep A	Vale of Leven	2-3
	Rd 3 H	Lochee Harp	1-1
	Rep A	Lochee Harp	4-2
	Rd 4 H	Largs Thistle	0-6
94/5	Rd 1 Bye		
	Rd 2 A	Kello Rovers	1-1
	Rep H	Kello Rovers	2-
2,		4-2 on pens	
	Rd 3 H	Carnoustie Panmure	2-2
	Rep A	Carnoustie Panmure	0-3
95/6	Rd 1 Bye		
	Rd 2 H	Balbeggie	2-0
	Rd 3 A	Scone Thistle	0-3
96/7	Rd 1 A	Dunbar United	0-2
97/8	Rd 1 Bye		
	Rd 2 H	Fauldhouse United	2-3
98/9	Rd 1 H	Bye	
	Rd 2 A	Johnstone Burgh	3-
599/0	Rd 1 Bye		
	Rd 2 A	Ardrossan Winton R	7-1
	Rd 3 A	Largs Thistle	0-1
00/1	Rd 1 Bye		
	Rd 2 H	Bo'ness United	2-2
	Rep A	Bo'ness United	1-
1,		4-3pens	
	Rd 3 H	Dundee North End	1-2
01/2	Rd 1 Bye		
	Rd 2 A	Johnstone Burgh	1-4
02/3	Rd 1 H	Johnstone Burgh	1-1
	Rep A	Johnstone Burgh	2-4
03/4	Rd 1 H	Shettleston	1-1
	Rep A	Shettleston	1-1
		5-6 on pens	
04/5	Rd 1 Bye		
	Rd 2 A	Banks o' Dee	2-1
	Rd 3 A	Beith	0-6
05/6	Rd 1 Bye		
	Rd 2 H	East Kilbride Thistle	0-3
06/7	Rd 1 Bye		
	Rd 2 H	Pollok	1-4

HONOURS	
Fife County League (West)	1938/9
Fife County League	1947/8, 1953/4, 1955/6, 1961/2, 1962/3, 1963/4
Fife Cup	1937/8, 1950/1, 1960/1, 1963/4, 1979/80
Cowdenbeath Cup	1952/3, 1955/6, 1961/2, 1963/4, 1967/8, 1974/5
Express Cup	1960/1, 1963/4
Kingdom Kegs Cup	2002/3
Mitchell Cup	1937/8, 1955/6, 1961/2, 1962/3
West Fife Cup	1937/8, 1938/9, 1948/9, 1953/4, 1954/5, 1962/3

TOP—A crowd behind the goal is a rare event. These are Pollok supporters during the 2006/7 Scottish Junior Cup tie.
MIDDLE– Welcome to Central Park. The Central Park pavilion pictured from outside the ground.
BELOW—Looking towards the new (ish) pavilion from the uncovered terracing side of Central Park. On a fine day this side provides the best vantage point in the ground. On a wet day stick to the covered terrace on the opposite side.

LUNCARTY

Ground— Brownlands Park, Luncarty
Ground Phone Number—
Postcode / GPS Location— PH1 3EP

Club Colours— Tangerine and Black

Club Secretary 2006/7— Ian Bannerman, 01738 629807

HISTORY
The date of formation for Luncarty FC is variously quoted at anything from 1886 to 1928! Doubtless football was played in the village from before the earlier date and the exact lineage of the various football teams may be hard to establish. In their own match programme for a Centenary Game against Dundee United in 1986 Luncarty claim that they were formed in 1886 by the employees of James Burt Marshall, Bleachers in the town. To this day the nickname applied to the team is 'The Bleachers'. That match programme contends that they have always played in Junior football but that they also competed in the Perthshire Senior Cup around the turn of the Century. The obvious answer would be that a Junior side continued in parallel with the Seniors in the early 20th Century - but perusal of a league table from the Perthshire Juniors for 1920/1 gives no indication of a Luncarty side. It may be that from such a long distance away in time the distinction between the Perthshire Junior and Senior Leagues has 'blurred'.

What seems clear is that Luncarty was represented in Perthshire Junior football from the early 1920s. The Junior club of that era may well have been the same team as the 'senior' Luncarty side which existed earlier. The date of 'conversion' to senior status is variously given as 1921 and 1923. The senior competed in the Scottish Qualifying Cup up to 1921/22 so 1922 would seem to be the earliest likely date of their switch to juniordom.

Langlands Park, in the centre of the village, was home to the team from its earliest days through until 1997. The only interruption was during World War Two when the ground was ploughed up for vegetable growing and the footballers decamped to Milton Park. In 1997 Luncarty moved to a new ground at Brownlands Park, adjacent to the main road and railway through the village.

Luncarty claim many names that have stepped up to senior level. "Ginger" Ewing of Manchester City, Eric Guthrie (Portsmouth), Sandy Wann (also Manchester City), Malcolm Darling (Blackburn Rovers) and Dougie Robb (Montrose) are prominent amongst them. Within the junior world the club were greatly honoured when club official George Millar was made President of the Scottish Junior FA in the 1960s.

It may say something about the nature of Luncarty to look at the team of 1946/7. It contained four sets of brothers and the three other team members were all related to one another!

Up until the 1960s the club were relatively successful within local circles. The amalgamation of the Perthshire League with the Dundee and Angus ones made life more difficult for them and results suffered.

In 1998/9 the club took a 'year out' to restructure but they did return one year later. 2006/7 was something of a red-letter year because the club actually won a Scottish Junior Cup tie. Forres Thistle were defeated 1-0 away from home to notch up the first win in the national competition for 20 years - since 1987/8 when Luncarty travelled to Bo'ness United and pulled off a massive shock by winning 3-1. Prior to that they had gone eleven seasons without a Cup win since beating Perth Celtic 3-1 in 1975/6!

GROUND
Luncarty moved from Langlands Park to Brownlands Park in 1997. The ground is unusual with the pavilion and social club located high above the playing field - players run down a flight of steps to reach the field. The far side of the ground is bounded by the huge embankment carrying the Perth to Inverness railway - this is outside the ground and not open to spectators. The best viewing angle is achieved from the end behind the goal at the Social Club. Otherwise the pitch is simply roped off with flat (and frequently wet) standing for the spectators.

SUPPORT
Luncarty is really just a small village and the locals do not get out to support the team. Bigger games may attract a few dozen locals but more typically the home support is in single figures.

GETTING THERE
It really could not be simpler to find Luncarty's ground. Leaving Perth on the A9 and heading north it is only a couple of miles until Luncarty is signposted. Take the turning and approach the village from the south. The ground is on the left, three-quarters way though the built up area. Coming from the north (Bankfoot) end of the village, the ground is obvious on the right as you enter.

Although the railway abuts the football ground there is no station at Luncarty. The village is served by the same bus services as go to Bankfoot from Perth (see Bankfoot Athletic section). Bankfoot is a further five minutes up the road.

PROGRAMMES
Luncarty issued a programme for their Centenary match against Dundee United in August 1986. They may not have issued any before then or since then.

WEBSITE

TEN YEAR LEAGUE RECORD
1996/7	Tayside League Div Two	10th out of 11	19pts
1997/8	Tayside League Div Two	11th out of 11	8pts
1998/9	In abeyance		
1999/00	Tayside League First Div	12th out of 12	4pts
2000/1	Tayside League First Div	11th out of 12	17pts

2001/2	Tayside League First Div	12th out of 12	12pts
2002/3	Tayside League First Div	7th out of 10	23pts
2003/4	Tayside League First Div	7th out of 10	24pts
2004/5	Tayside League First Div	4th out of 10	30pts
2005/6	Tayside League First Div	2nd out of 9	34pts

TOWN

Little more than a dormitory village for Perth. It was founded in 1782 by a William Sandeman to provide accommodation for workers on his bleachfield, the largest in Scotland. There are a few shops on the main road and a few more in the main part of the village which is located east of the road. The main A9 used to pass through here, much as it did at Bankfoot, but the building of the new version in the 1970s has left Luncarty a much quieter and more attractive place. The sport most often associated with the village is fishing. Some of the salmon beats on the River Tay next to the town are regarded as amongst the finest in the land.

SCOTTISH JUNIOR CUP RECORD

88/9	Rd 1	A	Largs Thistle	0-3
89/90	Rd 1	A	Forres Thistle	0-1
90/1	Rd 1	A	Preston Athletic	2-4
91/2	Rd 1	H	Bon Accord	0-13
92/3	Rd 1	A	Larkhall Thistle	2-4
93/4	Rd 1	Bye		
	Rd 2	A	Kirrie Thistle	1-5
94/5	Rd 1	H	Coupar Angus	0-4
95/6	Rd 1	Bye		
	Rd 2	A	Camelon	0-10
96/7	Rd 1	H	Sunnybank	0-1
97/8	Rd 1	Bye		
	Rd 2	H	Vale of Leven	0-8
98/9	In abeyance			
99/0	Rd 1	Bye		
	Rd 2	H	Maybole	1-3
00/1	Rd 1	Bye		
	Rd 2	A	Maud	1-3
01/2	Rd 1	Bye		
	Rd 2	A	Formartine United	1-7
02/3	Rd 1	A	Renfrew	0-2
03/4	Rd 1	A	Larkhall Thistle	1-7
04/5	Rd 1	A	Port Glasgow Athletic	1-1
	Rep	H	Port Glasgow Athletic	2-2, 0-3 on pens
05/6	Rd 1	A	Lesmahagow	0-1
06/7	Rd 1	Bye		
	Rd 2	A	Forres Thistle	1-0

HONOURS
Perthshire Junior League   1928/9, 1931/2, 1949/50, 1964/5
Tayside Regional League Division 2 1972/3, 1989/90
Constitutional Cup   1940/1, 1964/5
Currie Cup   1957/8
PA Cup   1963/4, 1971/2
Perthshire Junior Cup   1940/1, 1952/3, 1963/4

The Social Club (Top) sits high above the playing surface at Luncarty's trim little ground at Brownlands Park.

NEWBURGH

Ground— East Shore Park
Ground Phone Number—
Postcode / GPS Location— KY14 6BA

Club Colours— Black and White

Club Secretary 2006/7— Denise Roberts, 01337 827701

Newburgh is quite far removed from the rest of Fife. Since the merging of the Perth sides into the 'East Central' area in 2006, the north Fife side have had less travelling to do for games against the likes of Jeanfield Swifts.

HISTORY
The town of Newburgh, on the south shore of the River Tay, first saw Junior football in 1897/8. A team called Tayside Albion was based there and joined the Howe of Fife League – a few years later they switched to the Perth and District League to reduce their costs. The club folded in 1909. They were replaced by Newburgh West End who are the direct antecedents of the current club, who claim 1909 as their year of formation. Until World War One they played in the Perthshire Leagues and the Fife Cups. Between the wars they restricted themselves to Fife football but after World War Two they moved back to the Perthshire League. However, in 1962 they came back to the Fife fold and at the same time dropped the West End tag to become plain Newburgh Juniors. Newburgh were in abeyance for 1989/90 due to a lack of committee members but they returned a stronger team than before. The record crowd of 4106 was set for a Scottish Cup Quarter Final tie against Irvine Meadow in 1961/2 – Burgh reached the Semi Finals losing to Renfrew at Glasgow's Firhill Park in front of an attendance of 12770. Earlier in that Cup run a match against Armadale Thistle, also at Newburgh, had attracted a crowd of 2600.

Newburgh almost repeated the feat of reaching the Semi Final in 1971. They got as far as the Quarter Finals before Dalkeith Thistle put paid to their hopes with a 3-0 win.

The club honours list is longer than that of many comparable teams. This is partly because they have, at different times, switched between Perthshire and Fife competitions and have won most of them. Cursory perusal of the list reveals that their best days are a long time in the past.

Season 2006/7 was something of a paradox for Newburgh. Off the field the club seemed to be doing well with the ground being spruced up and a reasonable level of local interest. On the field, despite the experienced management team led by former Rangers, Dundee and Hearts player Cammy Fraser, results were awful. The first league win of the season was delayed until March 2007 by which time Fraser had been replaced by Kevin Huskie.

The club are ambitious to improve their status. They have applied for permission to develop the ground in a bid to attract the quality of players required for Super League football. The plan is to have a new club house in place by 2009. They have also tied up an agreement with Ladybank Violet Under 16s to be a 'feeder' club for the Juniors.

GROUND
East Shore Park is a real gem amongst football grounds and well worthy of a visit. The club own the ground having bought it in 1974 after a fund-raising campaign. This involved a mail drop to every home in the town requesting ten pounds towards the cost. As it's name suggests it is located close to the shore. Driving through Newburgh it is easy to forget that the river has been a major influence on the town. Small boats are moored and beached at Newburgh and from time to time larger coasters pass by as they access Perth Harbour. There are entrances at either end of the ground. The pavilion is located at the north (River Tay) end - the ground lies at 90 degrees to the river. Beside the pavilion is a large mound which affords the best view in the ground.

The east side has a small seated grandstand - something of a novelty for junior football. The south end is flat standing and there is terracing at the west side - where a considerable degree of shelter is provided by the trees that form the boundary between the ground and surrounding properties. This side also has a small covered enclosure as pictured above. The whole place has an ambiance which is more like a leafy English village than an outpost of northern Fife.

SUPPORT
Newburgh have a very loyal and committed group of supporters. Their travelling support numbers around twenty with about four times that number likely to attend most home games. The town has a real community-feel about it which reflects in the enthusiasm of their supporters.

GETTING THERE
Newburgh is relatively inaccessible but well worth making the effort to get to. By car leave the M90 Edinburgh-Perth motorway at Junction 9, close to Bridge of Earn. Take the A912 southwards for a mile or so, then take the A913. Pass through Aberargie and Abernethy and you will arrive in Newburgh after around ten minutes. The ground is between the main road and the Rover Tay towards the eastern end of the town. The pitch is actually visible down Tay Street at the eastern end of the High Street – go down this street and find a parking place. Approaching from the east, East Shore Park is at the end of the town you approach from – turn right down Tay Street.

Although the Edinburgh to Perth railway line passes through Newburgh the station is long since closed. The nearest railway stations are Perth, Ladybank and Cupar – Newburgh is roughly equidistant from all three. Bus services F1 and F2, from St Andrews to Newburgh pass through Cupar and provide an hourly service. Bus 35 links Perth, Newburgh and Cupar but the service is two-hourly at best. Bus services after midweek games are non-existent. Connections from Ladybank are not really worth considering.

PROGRAMMES
Newburgh did issue programmes for major Scottish Junior Cup ties back in the early 1960s but have rarely, if ever, produced them since then.

WEBSITE
Newburgh used to have a good website but it had disappeared in recent years. Happily this has been rectified and an excellent site is now on line at: http://www.newburghjfc.com
The site also has a fans forum.

TEN YEAR LEAGUE RECORD
1996/7	Fife League	7th out of 15	27pts
1997/8	Fife League	4th out of 15	61 pts
1998/9	Fife League	5th out of 16	58pts
1999/00	Fife League	5th out of 15	53pts
2000/1	Fife League	10th out of 15	36pts
2001/2	Fife League	10th out of 15	37pts
2002/3	Fife League	10th out of 12	19pts
2003/4	Fife League	8th out of 10	19pts
2004/5	Fife League	10th out of 12	21pts
2005/6	Fife League`	10th out of 13	26pts

TOWN (Population 2040)
The Fife town of Newburgh claims inhabitation for over 1000 years and this may well be a conservative guess! Just outside Mugdrum House there is a stone cross (standing 13ft high) of Celtic design. The carvings are considered to be more than 1300 years old. Although it now appears as a pillar, originally it most probably had arms as of a real cross.

Newburgh (or New Burgh by the Abbey of Lindores as it was then) received its Royal Charter from Alexander III in 1266, with later privileges granted by the Abbot of Lindores in 1457. The town was granted further privileges by both James VI and Charles I.

On a hill just a little way south of Newburgh, by the road leading to the Strathearn region of neighbouring Perthshire, stands the MacDuff Cross. Although badly damaged in 1559 by the Reformers, the cross is still very much a legendary place of sanctuary for all those of the MacDuff clan who had been involved in murder.

Such MacDuff clan members could achieve atonement by performing a series of rituals. Having touched the MacDuff stone, they would then wash themselves

SCOTTISH JUNIOR CUP RECORD				
88/9	Rd 1	H	Kirkcaldy YM	3-3
	Rep	A	Kirkcaldy YM	1-3
90/1	Rd 1	H	Irvine Vics	3-4
91/2	Rd 1	Bye		
	Rd 2	H	Kirkintilloch Rob Roy	2-5
92/3	Rd 1	Bye		
	Rd 2	A	Irvine Meadow	0-3
93/4	Rd 1	Bye		
	Rd 2	H	Maybole	3-2
	Rd 3	A	Beith	1-3
94/5	Rd 1	H	Dalkeith Thistle	1-1
	Rep	A	Dalkeith Thistle	2-3
95/6	Rd 1	H	Fochabers	7-1
	Rd 2	A	Hill of Beath Hawthorn	1-2
96/7	Rd 1	Bye		
	Rd 2	H	St Josephs	0-0
	Rep	A	St Josephs	2-2, 4-5 pens
97/8	Rd 1	Bye		
	Rd 2	A	Carnoustie Panmure	1-2
98/9	Rd 1	A	Carluke Rovers	1-2
99/0	Rd 1	Bye		
	Rd 2	A	Glenafton Athletic	2-4
00/1	Rd 1	A	Lochgelly Albert	3-1
	Rd 2	H	Kelty Hearts	2-4
01/2	Rd 1	Bye		
	Rd 2	H	East Craigie	2-1
	Rd 3	A	Whitburn	1-1
	Rep	H	Whitburn	0-2
02/3	Rd 1	A	Bankfoot Athletic	4-0
	Rd 2	H	Wilson's XI	6-2
	Rd 3	H	Penicuik Athletic	2-1
	Rd 4	H	Arthurlie	0-3
03/4	Rd 1	Bye		
	Rd 2	A	Kilsyth Rangers	0-2
04/5	Rd 1	Bye		
	Rd 2	A	Vale of Leven	2-3
05/6	Rd 1	Bye		
	Rd 2	H	FC Stoneywood	0-0
	Rep	A	FC Stoneywood	1-2
06/7	Rd 1	Bye		
	Rd 2	A	Coupar Angus	3-1
	Rd 3	A	Petershill	0-6

HONOURS
Fife County League   1924/5
Perthshire Junior League   1946/7, 1953/4, 1954/5, 1955/6, 1956/7
Fife Regional League   1972/3, 1976/7
Fife Cup   1932/3, 1952/3, 1961/2, 1964/5, 1966/7, 1969/70, 1973/4
Constitutional Cup   1950/1
Cowdenbeath Cup   1960/1, 1966/7, 1975/6
Currie Cup   1953/4, 1954/5
East Fife Cup   1923/4, 1936/7, 1965/6, 1972/3
Express Cup   1961/2, 1966/7
Mitchell Cup   1954/5, 1960/1, 1963/4, 1964/5
PA Cup   1949/50, 1953/4, 1954/5, 1957/8, 1958/9
Perthshire Rosebowl   1953/4, 1954/5, 1956/7 1962/3, 1968/9

nine times at nearby Ninewells. They would also have to pay a forfeit of nine cows!

The town lies immediately south of Mugdrum Island which divides the River Tay into the North and South Deeps. Reed cultivation and harvesting was a particular local industry until recently. Like Kirkcaldy, Newburgh also had a long association with the linoleum industry. That ended in 1980 when the Courtaulds Factory was gutted by fire.

The grandstand at East Shore Park, described on the club website as the 'home' stand. This is because Newburgh, in common with most junior clubs, have dug-outs (sorry, technical areas) on opposite sides of the field and the home one is on this side.

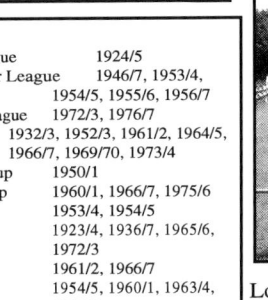

Looking northwards towards the pavilion end. Newburgh hope to have this replaced by 2009 to coincide with the club's Centenary year.

OAKLEY UNITED

Ground— Blairwood Park
Ground Phone Number—
Postcode / GPS Location— KY12 9QG

Club Colours— Sky Blue and Maroon

Club Secretary 2006/7— Douglas Hynd, 01383 851779

Oakley is now the westernmost outpost of Fife junior football following the demise of Tulliallan Thistle and Clackmannan Juniors. These two clubs both joined the Juniors at around the same time as Oakley United but have failed to survive. The fact that Oakley have not just survived but have prospered is down to he hard work of their committee men and the support of the local community.

HISTORY

A team called Oakley United played in the Clackmannanshire Junior League before World War One. They did not enjoy much success and quickly reverted to the juvenile level. They played at Foundry Park which is now the site of a Primary School. Immediately after World War Two Oakley United Juveniles shared the use of the ground with Junior team Comrie Colliery but when the land was taken over for building the school the Juniors moved to nearby Blairhall. Oakley Juveniles forged a link with Comrie Colliery and at some point played under the name of Comrie Colliery Juveniles using an open field located where Blairwood Park is today. Oakley United Juniors were formed at a Public Meeting on 5/4/64 when the Comrie Colliery Juvenile side changed their name back to Oakley United.

Oakley United joined the Fife Junior League. They spent their first season ground-sharing with Comrie Colliery at Blairhall before their own Blairwood Park was improved to junior standard.

It took more than ten years for Oakley to make much impact on the Scottish Junior Cup. In 1976/7 they got as far as Round 5 before succumbing to eventual semi-finalists Lesmahagow at Blairwood Park. Nine years later, in 1985/6, they went one further by reaching the Quarter Finals before losing 2-0 at Cumnock. That remains their best run in the national competition to date. Up until the 1990s Oakley were a fairly run-of-the-mill Fife League side. Since then they have emerged as one of the strongest and have consistently challenged for honours. In a pecking order they probably sit somewhere just behind Hill of Beath and Kelty, alongside Glenrothes, but ahead of the rest.

Over the years several well-known names have played for the club, including Cammy Fraser, George Connelly, Ernie McGarr, David Bingham, Raymond Sharp and Kenny Ward.

Player-manager Willie Newbigging, a former St Johnstone and Alloa player and a real stalwart of the juniors, lends his considerable experience to the side.

Oakley do have a reputation for developing younger players and they are less likely than some clubs to throw money at veteran ex-seniors. They have ambitions plans to upgrade the pavilion at Blairwood Park in line with their status in the game.

GROUND
For a team that has been relatively successful on the field in recent years, spectator facilities at Blairwood Park leave something to be desired. However, crowds are very poor here and the small covered enclosure on the south side of the ground is probably sufficient to shelter most people on a rainy day. The entrances are behind the east goal and are not immediately obvious from the main (or only) road passing through the village. Spectators have to go in behind the garages at the east end and they will find the gates.

All the standing areas are grassed. There is a steep embankment behind the east goal but the remainder of the ground is flat. Shelter from the wind is provided by some giant leylandii trees on the north side.

The ground was opened in 1965 - the land was purchased with the assistance of local miners who contributed £300 towards the cost. Until 1972 the ground was made up of flat standing but in that year the embankment behind the east goal was created. In 1985 new changing rooms, costing £15,000, were opened with a friendly match against a Glasgow Celtic XI. Prior to then a redundant pre-fab had been used for changing facilities.

SUPPORT
The villagers of Oakley will turn out in fair numbers for Cup ties but bread and butter matches see attendances of fewer than 100.

GETTING THERE
Oakley Station closed many years ago. The nearest railway service now is to Dunfermline.

This is another ground for which car transport is really the most viable option. From the Kincardine Crossing take the A977 towards Alloa, then the A907 from the Gartary Roundabout close to Clackmannan. Oakley is approximately 6 miles from this roundabout. Entering the village the road dips, and then rises with Blairwood Park on the left. The boundary wall is impressive with Blairwood Park emblazoned on it.

From the Forth Bridge (A90) take a left at Junction 1 of the M90 onto the A985, signposted for Kincardine. Carrying straight on through Rosyth and Crombie brings you to the Cairneyhill Roundabout. A minor road is signposted to Oakley from here. It is a twisty and narrow road but once in the centre of the village turn left at a T-Junction and Blairwood Park is on the right.

From the North, head for Dunfermline then follow the A907 signs. This will bring you into Oakley with Blairwood Park on the right in the middle of the village.

By bus Oakley is served regularly from Dunfermline. Services 74 and 75 run approximately half hourly and the journey takes just under 20 minutes. Predictably the bus and railway stations in Dunfermline are not especially close to each other.

PROGRAMMES

Oakley issued a programme for a match against Glasgow Celtic in the 1980s to open the new pavilion at Blairwood Park. This may be the only programme that the club have ever issued.

WEBSITE

Oakley United have one of the best-presented websites in Junior football. It can be accessed at: http://www.oakleyunited.co.uk

TEN YEAR LEAGUE RECORD

1996/7	Fife League	11th out of 15	25pts
1997/8	Fife League	3rd out of 15	62pts
1998/9	Fife League	6th out of 16	54pts
1999/0	Fife League	6th out of 15	51pts
2000/1	Fife League	1st out of 15	72pts
2001/2	Fife League	3rd out of 1	56pts P
2002/3	East Super L	7th out of 12	27pts
2003/4	East Super L	9th out of 12	25pts
2004/5	East Super L	10th out of 12	20pts R
2005/6	Fife League	1st out of 13	57pt P

TOWN

Originally associated with the Oakley Iron Works, which were established in 1846, the settlement was revitalised in the 1930s after the opening of the nearby Comrie Colliery coal mine. The white-harled Church of the Most Holy Name, notable for its magnificent stained glass windows and carved 'Stations of the Cross', was built to the south of the village in 1956-8 for Roman Catholic miners who had moved from Lanarkshire to work in the more prosperous coalfields of West Fife. The coal mine closed some years ago and there is now little employment in the village According to official statistics Oakley is now in the 15% of most deprived areas in Scotland.

SCOTTISH JUNIOR CUP RECORD

Season	Round	H/A	Opponent	Score
88/9	Rd 1	A	Glasgow Perthshire	3-1
	Rd 2	H	Leven	4-0
	Rd 3	H	Hill of Beath Hawthorn	2-1
	Rd 4	A	Kelty Hearts	0-0
	Rep	H	Kelty Hearts	0-1
89/90	Rd 1	H	Brechin Vics	4-0
	Rd 2	H	Burghead Thistle	8-0
	Rd 3	A	East Craigie	2-1
	Rd 4	A	Fauldhouse United	2-3
90/1	Rd 1	H	Montrose Roselea	2-2
	Rep	A	Montrose Roselea	3-3
	Rep	N	Montrose Roselea	0-1
91/2	Rd 1		Bye	
	Rd 2	H	Whitletts Vics	3-2
	Rd 3	H	Islavale	2-0
	Rd 4	A	Vale of Leven	0-2
92/3	Rd 1		Bye	
	Rd 2	H	Kello Rovers	2-3
93/4	Rd 1		Bye	
	Rd 2	H	Jeanfield Swifts	3-1
	Rd 3	H	Kirrie Thistle	1-3
94/5	Rd 1	A	Kinloss	5-0
	Rd 2	H	Arthurlie	0-7
95/6	Rd 1	H	Montrose Roselea	3-1
	Rd 2	A	Irvine Meadow	1-4
96/7	Rd1	H	Scone Thistle	1-2
97/8	Rd 1		Bye	
	Rd 2	H	Brechin Vics	2-1
	Rd 3	H	Johnstone Burgh	0-2
98/9	Rd 1		Bye	
	Rd 2	H	Ardrossan Winton Ro	0-0
	Rep	A	Ardrossan Winton Ro	2-3
99/0	Rd 1	H	Jeanfield Swifts	2-1
	Rd 2	A	Vale of Leven	2-2
	Rep	H	Vale of Leven	2-0
	Rd 3	A	Carnoustie Panmure	1-4
00/1	Rd 1		Bye	
	Rd 2	H	Forth Wanderers	3-1
	Rd 3	A	Greenock	5-1
	Rd 4	H	Petershill	0-1
01/2	Rd 1		Bye	
	Rd 2	H	Buckie Rovers	2-1
	Rd 3	H	Tulliallan Thistle	4-0
	Rd 4	A	Whitburn	3-1
	Rd 5	H	Auchinleck Talbot	3-3
	Rep	A	Auchinleck Talbot	3-5
02/3	Rd 1		Bye	
	Rd 2	H	Bonnybridge	4-2
	Rd 3	A	Camelon	1-2
03/4	Rd 1		Bye	
	Rd 2	A	Bo'ness United	1-4
04/5	Rd 1		Bye	
	Rd 2	A	Tranent	4-1
	Rd 3	H	Greenock	1-1
	Rep	A	Greenock	1-1.
			2-3 on pens	
05/6	Rd 1		Bye	
	Rd 2	A	Montrose Roselea	1-4
06/7	Rd 1		Bye	
	Rd 2	H	Girvan	8-0
	Rd 3	H	Rutherglen Glencairn	1-2

HONOURS

Fife Regional League 1971/2, 1978/9, 1979/80, 1985/6, 1987/8, 2000/1, 2005/6
Fife and Lothians Cup 1982/3
Fife Cup 1987/8
Cowdenbeath Cup 1970/1, 1982/3, 1995/6, 1998/9, 2001/2, 2003/4
Fife Dryborough Cup 1976/7, 1980/1, 1982/3
Kingdom Kegs Cup 2000/1, 2004/5
West Fife Cup 1968/9, 1972/3
Fife League Cup 2005/6

ROSYTH

Ground— Recreation Park
Ground Phone Number—
Postcode / GPS Location— KY11 2BN

Club Colours— Red and Black

Club Secretary 2006/7— Matt Lawson, 01592 262193

Following the name changes, and location changes, of Rosyth Juniors is a daunting task. The current team are an ambitious and well-organised outfit who have the potential for success. Three-quarters way though the 2006/7 they were challenging for promotion from the East Region Premier Division to the Super League.

HISTORY

Jubilee Athletic played in the Kirkcaldy and District Amateur League from 1960. Initially they played in Pitreavie Park (between Rosyth and Dunfermline) and the club was comprised of members of the Dunfermline Athletic Supporters Club. They later moved to McKane Park in Dunfermline itself. Turning Junior in 1964, they played at McKane Park until 1969/70. McKane Park, which was close to the Ladysmill grounds of the local rugby and cricket clubs, has since been redeveloped as housing. In 1969 the club proposed to play their home games at North End Park in Cowdenbeath, home of Cowdenbeath FC before the construction of Central Park. They remained there until 1972. However, the local council, who had taken over North End Park, refused permission for Jubilee to charge admission money so they looked elsewhere. For a short time they groundshared with Cowdenbeath FC and acted as an unofficial feeder team for the Second Division side in 1972/3. In 1973 Jubilee Athletic groundshared with Castlehill Colliery at Woodside Park in the West Fife village of Blairhall. In 1973 they found their own base at Ballast Bank in Inverkeithing, former home of a team called Caldwell's Paper Mills. To begin with facilities for players were rudimentary but they gradually improved- for spectators their never were any facilities. In 1989 Jubilee moved to the well-appointed Pitreavie Sports Stadium, a stones throw from their original home at the local Playing Fields. The stadium was not ideal for football with a very narrow pitch and being surrounded by an athletics track. It took a Court case to gain permission to play there after opposition from local athletes. In 1992 the club changed its name to Rosyth Recreation and took over their present ground in Rosyth. For a spell in the early 90s the club were managed by former Dunfermline Athletic boss Jim Leishman who was out of senior football at the time – he later returned to East End Park as manager and general manager. Rosyth can also count Dick Campbell and Bert Paton amongst their former managers- both well-known names in Scottish football. The latter part of their name was dropped in 2006 leaving them as plain Rosyth FC.

But the history of Jubilee Athletic is just one strand in the story of junior football in Rosyth. A Junior team called Rosyth Recreation was formed in 1916 and continued for ten years in the Fife Juniors. In 1919 a senior club called Rosyth Dockyard Recreation was formed and ran parallel with the Juniors for a while. When the Junior team went into abeyance in 1926 the senior side were the town's only football representatives. Rosyth Dockyard Recreation were one of several amateur clubs around Scotland associated with major employers an companies. Senior status meant they could compete in the Scottish Qualifying Cup and potentially the Scottish Cup itself. For league fixtures they played in various competitions including the Edinburgh and District League. The senior team folded just before the start of World War Two. A club was re-formed as Juniors in 1946 and played in the Fife League and cups until 1957 when they went into abeyance. It is not fully clear whether this was a revival of either of the former senior or junior sides, or a totally new outfit. Although the website of the current junior side refers to these previous Rosyth teams as if they are the same club, the reality is that the family tree of football in Rosyth is very complicated indeed.

The current squad includes highly experienced men with a pedigree at a higher level.

The name Rosyth Recreation is now used by an Under 21 Juvenile club.

GROUND
Recreation Park in Rosyth is not a bad venue at which to watch football. It encloses a large area and several thousand people could see a match here without serious overcrowding. Most of the few that do choose to stand on the north side where a row of slabs has thoughtfully been laid to keep your feet dry. On the three other sides of the ground underfoot conditions can be marshy especially at the south east corner. Both ends have steep embankments with a few metal crush barriers 'planted' in them – they provide something to lean on when the weather is fine. The south side of the ground is a steep grassy embankment but is devoid of any spectator facilities. Catering is from a window on the end of a shed close to the entrances.

The previous incarnation of Rosyth Recreation also played at a ground called Recreation Park in the 1920s and again in the 1940s and 50s. No trace of the old ground remains. The senior club, known as Rosyth Dockyard Recreation, played on the Playing Fields now occupied by the Civil Service Sports Association, adjacent to Recreation Park.

SUPPORT
Rosyth are one of the few clubs to publish attendances in their excellent match programme. They average around the 80-100 mark for home games so probably have a hard core home support of around 60-70.

GETTING THERE
Rosyth Railway Station is half a mile from the ground along King's Road. It is on the Fife Circle, served by trains from Edinburgh to Dunfermline and Cowdenbeath. Exiting the station, make sure to take King's Road which runs

down the back of the Tesco supermarket rather than Queensferry Road which passes the front.

By car, and approaching from either the Forth Bridge or the M90 from Perth, take the A985 at Junction 1 of the M90. This is signposted for Kincardine. Recreation Park is on the left as you pass through Rosyth, behind a pub currently called 'The Yard'.

From the Kincardine Crossing, take the A985 towards the Forth Bridge. Recreation Park is one of the first things you will approach in Rosyth - on the right as you enter the town.

PROGRAMMES
Rosyth put most of their rivals to shame by issuing a programme for all home games. Full of information, it is one of the best in the country.

WEBSITE
The club have an informative website at:
http://www.rosythfc.co.uk

TEN YEAR LEAGUE RECORD
1996/7	Fife League	12th out of 15	23pts	
1997/8	Fife League	8th out of 15	34pts	
1998/9	Fife League	7th out of 16	51pts	
1999/00	Fife League	10th out of 15	30pts	
2000/1	Fife League	11th out of 15	28pts	
2001/2	Fife League	11th out of 15	32pts	
2002/3	Fife League	9th out of 12	24pts	
2003/4	Fife League	4th out of 10	30pts	
2004/5	Fife League	2nd out of 12	52pts	
2005/6	Fife League	3rd out of 13	49pts	Promoted

TOWN
Rosyth (pronounced Ross-sythe) (Scottish Gaelic: *Ros Saidhe* or *Ros Saoithe*) has the only direct ferry service to the European mainland from Scotland. The area is best known for its large dockyard, formerly the Royal Naval Dockyard Rosyth, construction of which began in 1909. The town was planned as a garden city with accommodation for the construction workers and dockyard workers. Today, the dockyard is almost 1,300 acres (5 km²) in size, a large proportion of which was reclaimed during construction. The associated naval base closed in 1994, and no Royal Navy ships are permanently based at Rosyth, though there are frequent visitors. Rosyth's dockyards became the very first in the Royal Navy to be privatised when Babcock International acquired the site in 1987. The privatisation followed almost a century of contribution to the defence of the United Kingdom which spanned two World Wars and the Cold War with the Soviet Union, during which Rosyth became a key nuclear submarine maintenance establishment. An overnight ferry service links Rosyth with Zeebrugge in Belgium once every other day.

Scottish Enterprise Fife is now working in partnership with various private sector organisations to explore the future development of Rosyth. The agency is looking at ways to expand the ferry services to other European and domestic ports. It also wants to help create new business infrastructure in and around Rosyth – which in turn will bring economic benefits to Fife and beyond.

Three areas around the port of Rosyth are being developed: Surplus land and buildings owned by engineering giant Babcock, which operates the naval dockyard, is being offered to external companies. The new Rosyth Business Park offers existing office and warehouse space – and the opportunity for custom-built properties. The main dock area – operated by Forth Ports – is ripe for further development. Since opening in 1997, the port has seen rising timber and cargo vessels use the facility. Its warehouse and logistics facilities make an ideal choice for exporters and importers. A site owned by Teesmuir/Teesland is being developed into an £80 million business park – called Rosyth Europarc. More than 13,000 square meters of office and hi-tech manufacturing have already been developed. Companies like Intelligent Finance and Bank of Scotland are on site. To complement these developments, a new £8.4 million road has been built to provide an enhanced link to the nearby M90 motorway. Computer printer firm Lexmark recently closed its manufacturing plant situated in Rosyth, with the loss of 700 jobs.

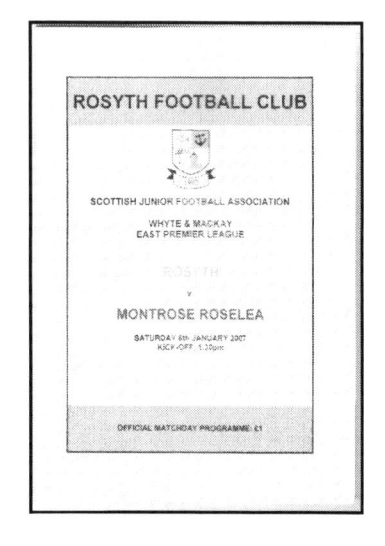

HONOURS		
ROSYTH RECREATION (1)		
Fife County League	1949/50	
Fife Cup	1948/9, 1949/50	
Cowdenbeath Cup	1949/50	
West Fife Cup	1923/4	
JUBILEE ATHLETIC		
Fife Cup	1980/1	
Cowdenbeath Cup	1980/1, 1987/8	

SCOTTISH JUNIOR CUP RECORD			
88/9	Rd 1	Bye	
	Rd 2 A	Penicuik Athletic	3-2
	Rd 3 H	Dundee North End	2-5
89/90	Rd 1	Bye	
	Rd 2 H	Blantyre Vics	2-2
	Rep A	Blantyre Vics	1-2
90/1	Rd 1 A	Stonehouse Violet	0-1
91/2	Rd 1	Bye	
	Rd 2 H	Lanark United	2-2
	Rep A	Lanark United	0-3
92/3	Rd 1	Bye	
	Rd 2 A	Blantyre Celtic	3-2
	Rd 3 A	Irvine Meadow	2-1
	Rd 4 H	Bathgate Thistle	1-2
93/4	Rd 1 A	Glenrothes	0-1
94/5	Rd 1 A	Johnstone Burgh	1-1
	Rep H	Johnstone Burgh	2-3
95/6	Rd 1	Bye	
	Rd 2 H	Lanark United	3-0
	Rd 3 H	Carluke Rovers	3-3
	Rep A	Carluke Rovers	1-2
96/7	Rd 1 A	Blairgowrie	4-3
	Rd 2 H	Islavale	5-1
	Rd 3 H	Arniston Rangers	0-3
97/8	Rd 1	Bye	
	Rd 2 A	Kirrie Thistle	1-2
98/9	Rd 1	Bye	
	Rd 2 H	Larkhall Thistle	1-2
99/0	Rd 1 A	Armadale Thistle	0-1
00/1	Rd 1 H	Pollok	1-7
01/2	Rd 1 A	Forfar West End	0-0
	Rep H	Forfar West End	3-1
	Rd 2 H	Dalkeith Thistle	0-1
02/3	Rd 1	Bye	
	Rd 2 H	Blackburn United	1-3
03/4	Rd 1	Bye	
	Rd 2 A	Blantyre Victoria	1-2
04/5	Rd 1	Bye	
	Rd 2 H	Turriff United	0-1
05/6	Rd 1	Bye	
	Rd 2 H	Ballingry Rovers	4-2
	Rd 3 H	Glasgow Perthshire	3-4
06/7	Rd 1	Bye	
	Rd 2 A	Lochee Harp	0-1

ABOVE—Four views of Recreation Park in Rosyth. BELOW, clockwise from top right, Burnside Park, Kincardine with the now-demolished Power Station in the background; Culross's football park which played home to the final days of Valleyfield Colliery; Picturesque Clackmannan with King George V Park in the foreground; Inverkeithing's Ballast Bank, erstwhile home of Jubilee Athletic

SCONE THISTLE

Ground— Robert Douglas Memorial Ground
Ground Phone Number—
Postcode / GPS Location—PH2 6RS

Club Colours— Red and white

Club Secretary 2006/7— Scott Stewart, 01738 812 841

HISTORY

The name of Scone Thistle dates back to 1882 and this is the year that the club takes as its point of foundation. It seems that the original club disbanded fairly soon afterwards. They returned to the Juniors in 1903. A senior club existed in the town between 1899 and 1922., competing in the Qualifying Cup competition with very limited success.

The Junior side were one of the top clubs in Perthshire throughout the 1930s. They won a host of local trophies although they did not make much of an impact on the national scene. Scone Thistle dropped out of the Juniors around the time of the Second World War and they remained in Amateur football until 1984.

The club's most famous former player must surely be the late George Best of Northern Ireland and Manchester United fame. When Best played in a charity event in Scone Thistle strip at Burrelton Park, a few miles north of Scone, in the summer of 1982, it was reported to be "like seeing a pink flamingo wading across the River Tay." Best's girlfriend, beauty-pageant queen Mary Stavin, also turned up and managed to make an impression. "You would expect Miss World to be stuck-up," said Scone Thistle honorary president Scott Farquharson. "Nothing was further from the truth. She sat at the side of the pitch chewing blades of grass, talking to my wife." Best came on in the charity fixture against Scone Amateurs with 20 minutes remaining. He scored to make it 14–0. The tournament also included local team Coupar Angus (for whom Scottish 60s hero Alan Gilzean had once played) and Vale of Atholl from Pitlochry (coached by a green newcomer called Paul Sturrock, then enjoying a fine playing career with Dundee Utd). Best then went on to play for Arbroath Vics taking part in a centenary match at Gayfield against Arbroath FC, and scoring twice in a 4-3 win for his "team for the day".

The reason for his appearances was, quite simply, money. He had been hit with an income tax bill which required full and quick settlement and he was able to command appearance fees which helped him to clear the debt. Reports from the time suggest that George Best appeared genuinely interested in the local football teams for which he played, and he made himself available after the games to talk to anyone who wanted an audience with him. Best and Stavin attended the Aerodrome Inn in Scone and then moved on to Murrayshall Hotel where Best held court at the bar. He was drinking heavily, but nothing stronger than tea!

Two years after Best's appearance for the club they made a welcome return to the Junior scene.

Philip Scott was farmed out to Scone Thistle from St Johnstone in 1990 prior to embarking on a senior career that took him to Sheffield Wednesday where his further progress was blighted by injury.

Scone Thistle won promotion from the Tayside Premier Division to the East Premier League for 2006/7.

GROUND

The Robert Douglas Memorial Ground is probably the lest-developed venue described in this book. Apart from a hatch in the pavilion wall selling the usual pies and drinks there are no spectator facilities in this ground at all. The ground is a large playing field with a metal rail surrounding the pitch. Entry is along a path and through a gate - the remainder of the ground is barely enclosed at all. It would be perfectly possible to effect entry over the loosely strung wire fence on the west side of the ground or indeed to watch for free from outside the supposed enclosure. This would be a travesty against the hard work put in by the Scone committee to keep their club going. For 2006/7 they climbed to the East Premier League although the signs were that they would be heading straight back to the more parochial environment of the Eats Region's North League. Spectators should be warned that underfoot conditions can be very boggy so go prepared with suitable footwear.

It is frequently asserted that the ground is named after the man who discovered the Douglas Fir. This is not the case. The Douglas Fir was named after David Douglas, brother of the Robert Douglas in question. The Robert Douglas after whom the ground is named is not, unsurprisingly, the former Celtic and Scotland goalkeeper last heard of languishing in Leicester City's reserve side. The Robert Douglas of Scone fame was born in the village in 1859. His father owned a large jam factory in the village but the young Robert Douglas emigrated to the United States. He made his fortune in the jam industry, becoming president of the Certo Corporation, and is credited with the discovery of pectin as a setting agent. When he died in 1929 he left $5 million to be spent on his home village of Scone. Some of that money was spent on building the school which stands next to the Playing Field, and on the field itself.

SUPPORT
Scone are a poorly-supported club. Home attendances will struggle to break the 30 mark, plus whatever the visiting side bring.

GETTING THERE
The nearest railway station is at Perth. Various bus services connect the town to Scone, notably the 3, 7, 57 and 58. By road the ground is not that easy to access from the motorway network. Leave the M90 / A90 at the north end of the Friarton Bridge and double back into Perth. Keep straight on at the traffic lights with the River Tay on your left. After the second road bridge the road splits. Take the right hand fork for Coupar Angus and Forfar. Scone is about

two miles away. To get to the Robert Douglas Memorial Ground turn left at the Wheel Inn into Stormont Road. The ground is a couple of hundred yards along this road on the right, after an imposing looking Primary School.

PROGRAMMES
Scone Thistle are one of the sides who produce a regular match programme. It is full of information and provides an excellent souvenir of a visit to the Robert Douglas Memorial Ground.

WEBSITE
There is no active Scone Thistle website at present.

TEN YEAR LEAGUE RECORD
1996/7	Tayside League Div One	12th out of 14	22pts	Relegated
1997/8	Tayside League Div Two	3rd out of 11	40pts	
1998/9	Tayside League First Div	6th out of 12	32pts	
1999/00	Tayside League First Div	9th out of 12	22pts	
2000/1	Tayside League First Div	8th out of 12	30pts	
2001/2	Tayside League First Div	5th out of 12	35pts	
2002/3	Tayside League First Div	1st out of 10	43pts	Promoted
2003/4	Tayside Premier Div	6th out of 11	22pts	
2004/5	Tayside Premier Div	6th out of 11	26pts	
2005/6	Tayside Premier Div	3rd out of 10	36pts	Promoted

TOWN (Population 4500)
The name of Scone is synonymous with Scottish history. However, the place which has such a deserved place in the nation's history is Old Scone, a couple of miles away from New Scone, home of Scone Thistle FC. Old Scone was the capital of the Pictish lands of Scotland from around 710. When Kenneth McAlpin assassinated the Pictish nobility in 843 as part of his scheme to enlarge his Kingdom of Alba he made Old Scone his capital. AT this time the Stone of Destiny was brought to Scone as the coronation stone for future Scots monarchs.

During the 12th Century Perth grew as a rival to Scone in trading and legal terms. When the invading English removed the Stone of Destiny to Westminster in 1296 Scone's days of pre-eminence were over. It remained primarily as a small weaving and bleaching settlement and was also the location of an Abbey. The latter was ransacked by a mob from Perth in 1559.

Between 1802 and 1812 the Earl of Mansfield, by then the owner of the land around Scone, wanted to develop his own private estate and Palace. The village of Old Scone stood in his way so he forcibly removed its population to a new location two miles away at 'New Scone'.

The new village had good quality housing and grew into a suburb of Perth. In the 1920s it was linked to Perth by an electric tramway.

Scone Aerodrome (or Perth Airport as it prefers to be known today) became a major training centre for pilots. Today Scone is a pleasant enough dormitory suburb of Perth with an affluent air about it.

SCOTTISH JUNIOR CUP RECORD			
88/9	Rd 1 Bye		
	Rd 2 A	Hurlford United	0-7
89/90	Rd 1 A	Dalry Thistle	2-3
90/1	Rd 1 Bye		
	Rd 2 H	Ashfield	1-10
91/2	Rd 1 A	Coupar Angus	3-1
	Rd 2 A	Aberdeen East End	0-1
92/3	Rd 1 A	Lochee United	2-5
93/4	Rd 1 Bye		
	Rd 2 H	Glasgow Perthshire	0-2
94/5	Rd 1 Bye		
	Rd 2 H	Forfar Albion	2-0
	Rd 3 A	Arthurlie	1-3
95/6	Rd 1 Bye		
	Rd 2 H	Vale of Clyde	2-0
	Rd 3 H	Lochore Welfare	3-0
	Rd 4 A	Glenrothes	2-2
	Rep H	Glenrothes	1-2
96/7	Rd 1 A	Oakley United	2-1
	Rd 2 H	Bonnybridge	3-2
	Rd 3 A	Stoneyburn	2-2
	Rep H	Stoneyburn	1-2
97/8	Rd 1 A	Aberdeen East End	1-3
98/9	Rd 1 Bye		
	Rd 2 H	Buchanhaven Hearts	2-2
	Rep A	Buchanhaven Hearts	1-4
99/0	Rd 1 Bye		
	Rd 2 H	Petershill	1-7
00/1	Rd 1 H	Rutherglen Glencairn	4-10
01/2	Rd 1 A	Bankfoot Athletic	2-1
	Rd 2 A	Tayport	0-2
02/3	Rd 1 Bye		
	Rd 2 H	Irvine Meadow	0-6
03/4	Rd 1 Bye		
	Rd 2 H	Vale of Leven	0-3
04/5	Rd 1 A	Livingston United	1-2
05/6	Rd 1 A	Thorniewood United	2-3
06/7	Rd 1 A	Aberdeen East End	0-1

HONOURS
East Region Tayside District League Division
One 2002/3
Tayside Regional League Division 2 1994/5
Tayside League Cup   2005/6
Perthshire Junior League   1920/1, 1923/4,
    1932/3, 1934/5, 1935/6
Currie Cup   1924/5, 1927/8, 1932/3
PA Cup   1929/30, 1931/2, 1935/6
Perthshire Junior Charity Cup   1923/4,
    1927/8, 1934/5
Perthshire Junior Cup 1925/6, 1927/8, 1928/9,
    1929/30, 1930/1, 1935/6

REL8 MEDIA

Rel8 Media have a range of titles planned covering aspects of football and football history in Scotland.

Coming soon are:

Regional History of Football in Scotland—a county by county study of the clubs, results, cups, leagues, players and grounds, covering Senior and Junior football

Non League Football in Scotland (East) Vol 2—Junior Football in the Lothians

Non League Football in Scotland (East) Vol 3—Junior Football in Dundee and Angus

For more details contact us by e-mail at: rel8med@btinternet.com

Or by post at: PO Box 29145, Dunfermline, Fife, KY12 7WJ

ST ANDREW'S UNITED

Ground— Recreation Park
Ground Phone Number—01334 477365
Postcode / GPS Location—KY16 8BN

Club Colours— Black and white

Club Secretary 2006/7— Kenneth Morris, 01334 476816

St Andrews is famous for two things and football is not one of them. Golf may not be everyone's idea of pleasurable leisure but it dominates the economy of St Andrews, along with the seat of learning that is the University of St Andrews. Shunned by most Scots, it is rather unfairly seen as a haven for failed Oxbridge wannabes studying esoteric subjects and spending mummy and daddy's money. Few make it along to see St Andrew's United, who play in the other part of town, seldom seen by tourists.

HISTORY
The town of St Andrews has been represented in Fife Junior football since the 1890s. Teams such as Ancient City Athletic, St Andrews City, St Andrews Violet, St Andrews Athletic and St Andrews Merchantiles are all known to have been active before World War One. After the War St Andrews Comrads were established at Links Park but the first mention of St Andrews United was in 1919/20, playing at Lade Braes Park. By 1922/3 United had moved to Recreation Park, their present home, where they have remained ever since.

The club's excellent website suggests that there have been three 'purple patches' in the history of St Andrews United. The first was in the late 1920s when they won the Fife Cup for two years in succession as well as winning several other local competitions.

Season 1959/60 was without doubt the best-ever for the club. They reached the Final of the Scottish Junior Cup and defeated Greenock Juniors 3-1 in the Final at Hampden Park. A crowd of 34,603 watched the Hampden Final against Greenock; he attendance of 15411 for the Semi Final against Thornton Hibs at Kirkcaldy was just as remarkable. It is fascinating to note that the team who played in the Final were a one-off eleven - they had never lined up together before nor did they do so afterwards! This second 'purple patch' extended into the mid 1960s with the club winning several other local competitions. These included the Fife League in 1964/5, so denying Lochore Welfare a record breaking fourth consecutive title.

The club then went into a period of decline and they almost folded in the early 1970s. By the late 1980s they had turned things around and had a team that embarked on a good period of trophy-winning. In 1989/90 the club lost just three out of 60 games all season. Since then they have maintained a good record and in 2006 they qualified for the new East Region Premier Division. The club are regarded as one of the most ambitious and progressive in the region. They also appear to have the resources to fund the signing of good quality players. 'Stars' from other Fife clubs have been persuaded to sign for St Andrews—it must be presumed that the Social Club provides an income stream that can support the payment of good signing on fees and wages.

GROUND
Recreation Park was opened in 1922 with St Andrew's United as the tenants. For a spell in the 1930s they shared the ground with St Andrew's Athletic - another Junior side. An enclosure was built on the east side of Recreation Park in 1953. This was later converted to a small seated stand which survived until the late 1990s when it was removed. When United's lease for the park expired in 1958 they attempted unsuccessfully to purchase the ground from the Local Council. Plans to build houses on the Recreation Park site came to nothing and United play there until this day.

The record attendances at the ground were set in 1960/1 during one of St Andrew's excellent Scottish Cup runs - the figure quoted for a replay against Armadale Thistle was 3000 and this is reckoned to be the highest. A more precise figure of 2895 has been reported for a match against Greenock during the same season.

Spectator viewing was improved on the east side of the ground when extra banking was built up from rubble and earth removed from a building site around this time.

United finally bought the ground in 1981 for £5000. A new pavilion was built shortly afterwards and the opening was celebrated with a match against Dundee United.

Entry is made from the west side at either end of the ground. This side is a mainly covered enclosure although there are only a few steps of shallow terracing to enhance viewing. The changing rooms are behind the north goal and there is little room for spectator accommodation except at the north-east corner. The grass banking on the east side gives the best view of the game provided the elements are kind. There is a large Social Club at the south end of the ground. Food is served from a hatch on the outside of the Social Club.

The ground is immaculately maintained and reflects the real pride that local people have in their side. Of all the Fife grounds this is one of the few that could easily make the transition to senior football.

SUPPORT
Compared to most clubs in the area St Andrews have a reasonable support. Crowds of over 100 are the norm for home games; and upwards of 20 will travel to away matches. Unlike some other venues the crowd is not entirely comprised of friends and relatives of the players. The match programme is one of the few to give accurate attendance figures (indeed, any attendance figures) for matches at this level and this confirms that Saints are one of the best-supported teams in the region. Promotion to the Premier League has not had much of an effect on attendances—most visiting sides do not carry a significant support.

GETTING THERE
The fact that St Andrew's is not on the railway is one of the more scandalous consequences of the Beeching cuts in the 1960s. The last train to St Andrew's ran in 1964. Nowadays the nearest railhead is at Leuchars on the Dundee to Edinburgh line. There are local bus services from there to St Andrew's but the town is best served by regular Express bus services from Edinburgh, Glasgow and Dundee.

By road, St Andrew's is well signposted. Most drivers will approach along the A91 from the west. After entering the town turn right onto the A915, signposted for Leven. After about three-quarters of a mile turn left into Lamond Drive. Recreation Park is about 400 yards away on the left.

PROGRAMMES
For the past few years St Andrews have produced an excellent matchday programme. It contains everything you would want from a good programme and is well-presented with full colour on the cover.

WEBSITE
St Andrews also have an excellent website reflecting the importance of good public relations to this progressive club. It can be found at:
http://www.webteams.co.uk/home.asp?team=standrewsutd

The website credits the same person as Programme Editor / Webmaster. It is to be hoped that he maintains his interest as the standard of both is excellent.

TEN YEAR LEAGUE RECORD
1996/7	Fife League	6th out of 15	31pts	
1997/8	Fife League	6th out of 15	48pts	
1998/9	Fife League	9th out of 16	38pts	
1999/00	Fife League	8th out of 15	37pts	
2000/1	Fife League	5th out of 15	54pts	
2001/2	Fife League	7th out of 15	49pts	
2002/3	Fife League	5th out of 12	32pts	
2003/4	Fife League	2nd out of 10	34pts	
2004/5	Fife League	6th out of 12	32pts	
2005/6	Fife League	2nd out of 13	55pts	Promoted

TOWN (Population 14,600)
The major attractions of St Andrews are well enough known and there is no need to go in great detail here. Suffice to say that if your boat is floated by things golfing then this is the place for you. The large number of well-heeled visitors, combined with the presence of a student population that is also comparatively affluent, means St Andrew's has a bewildering array of cafes, restaurants and the like. It's not a cheap place to stay or go out in but there is an excellent choice.

The University is located in buildings dotted around the town. This is far from the red-brick campus style universities of the 1960s and 70s! St Andrews University was founded in 1411 and has an ambiance and atmosphere more usually associated with Oxford and Cambridge.

In 1764 the world's first 18-hole Golf Course was opened at St Andrew's Links. This formalised the rules of golf at the St Andrew's Golf Club. In 1834 the club rather pompously changed its name to the 'Royal and Ancient Golf Club'.

Of course there is more to St Andrew's than golf, tourists and students. However, there is no denying that these dominate the local economy providing the bulk of employment for local people.

SCOTTISH JUNIOR CUP RECORD			
88/9	Rd 1 A	Dunipace	0-1
89/90	Rd 1 Bye		
	Rd 2 H	Downfield	1-1
	Rep A	Downfield	1-3
90/1	Rd 1 Bye		
	Rd 2 A	Ardeer Thistle	2-2
	Rep H	Ardeer Thistle	5-1
	Rd 3 H	Tayport	1-2
91/2	Rd 1 Bye		
	Rd 2 H	Buchanhaven Hearts	3-0
	Rd 3 H	Saltcoats Vics	4-0
	Rd 4 A	Arbroath SC	2-3
92/3	Rd 1 Bye		
	Rd 2 A	Bellshill Athletic	0-1
93/4	Rd 1 Bye		
	Rd 2 H	Lewis United	2-1
	Rd 3 A	Kilwinning Rangers	1-3
94/5	Rd 1 Bye		
	Rd 2 H	Musselburgh Athletic	1-1
	Rep A	Musselburgh Athletic	1-0
	Rd 3 A	Kirkintilloch Rob Roy	0-1
95/6	Rd 1 Bye		
	Rd 2 A	Neilston	3-1
	Rd 3 A	Dunipace	1-0
	Rd 4 A	Inverurie Loco Works	1-1
	Rep H	Inverurie Loco Works	0-2
96/7	Rd 1 H	Coltness United	2-1
	Rd 2 H	Carnoustie Panmure	0-5
97/8	Rd 1 Bye		
	Rd 2 H	St Rochs	1-0
	Rd 3 A	Harthill Royal	1-1
	Rep H	Harthill Royal	1-2
98/9	Rd 1 Bye		
	Rd 2 A	Kinnoull	1-0
	Rd 3 A	Montrose Roselea	0-1
99/0	Rd 1 H	Banks o' Dee	1-4
00/1	Rd 1 Bye		
	Rd 2 A	Carnoustie Panmure	0-4
01/2	Rd 1 H	Sunnybank	2-3
02/3	Rd 1 H	Dyce	5-1
	Rd 2 A	Bo'ness United	0-7
03/4	Rd 1 Bye		
	Rd 2 A	FC Stoneywood	1-1
	Rep H	FC Stoneywood	2-1
	Rd 3 H	Glenrothes	0-1
04/5	Rd 1 H	Downfield	0-0
	Rep A	Downfield	3-1
	Rd 2 A	Ardeer Thistle	4-1
	Rd 3 A	Tayport	0-3
05/6	Rd 1 Bye		
	Rd 2 H	Strathspey Thistle	3-2
	Rd 3 A	Vale of Clyde	2-1
	Rd 4 A	Bellshill Athletic	2-0
	Rd 5 A	Beith	1-5
06/7	Rd 1 Bye		
	Rd 2 A	Stonehaven	2-3

HONOURS	
Scottish Junior Cup	1959/60
Fife County League	1926/7, 1927/8, 1928/9, 1959/60, 1960/1, 1964/5
Fife Regional League	1989/90
Fife and Lothians Cup	1994/5
Fife Cup	1926/7, 1927/8, 1928/9, 1959/60, 1965/6, 1988/9, 1989/90
Cowdenbeath Cup	1957/8, 1965/6, 1968/9, 1990/1
East Coast Windows Cup	1987/8, 1988/9, 1989/90
East Fife Cup	1926/7, 1927/8, 1928/9
Express Cup	1958/9
Fife Shield	1926/7, 1927/8, 1928/9
Laidlaw Shield	1988/9
Mitchell Cup	1952/3, 1956/7, 1965/6 (shared)
Martin-White Cup	1920/1, 1921/2, 1924/5, 1925/6, 1926/7, 1927/8, 1935/6, 1936/7, 1937/8, 1938/9
West Fife Cup	1958/9, 1960/1, 1961/2, 1963/4
Peddie Smith Maloco Cup	2004/5
Kingdom Kegs Cup	2005/6

STEELEND VICTORIA

Ground— Woodside Park
Ground Phone Number—
Postcode / GPS Location—KY12 9LX

Club Colours— Blue

Club Secretary 2006/7—Hugh McQuillan, 01383 853181

Steelend is a tiny former mining settlement high in the West Fife hills close to the borders with Clackmannanshire and Perthshire. It is really an adjunct to the slightly larger but still relatively insignificant village of Saline. Steelend Vics have been around for a while although not always as a junior team. Their ground, at Woodside Park, was also used by Comrie Colliery for a while in the 1970s and 80s.

HISTORY
Steelend Victoria were accepted into the Fife Junior League for season 1946/47. In 1963 Steelend changed their name to Comrie Colliery to take advantaged of funding from miners at that pit - the previous incarnation of Comrie Colliery, based at Blairhall had gone defunct. In 1988, following the closure of the colliery, the club dropped out of junior football for a spell but returned in 1995 under their old name of Steelend Vics. Success has been hard to come by. The old club won the Fife League in 1951 and also lifted a couple of local Cups around that time. Comrie Colliery were less successful and the re-formed Steelend Vics have been regular strugglers in the Fife League. Their first six seasons back in the juniors never saw them escape from the bottom two. In 1999/2000 they managed to pick up a meagre two points all season. In more recent times there have signs of some progress with a younger team and a few very creditable results.

GROUND
Woodside Park must be the most exposed and open ground in Scotland. Such is the altitude that even when the sun is shining nearby, Steelend has its own micro-climate of mist, rain and damp. They are truly hardy folk who live there!

The ground was enclosed in 1947 but by the mid 1970s it was in a dilapidated state. Officials judged that it was no longer enclosed and Comrie Colliery had to move some Scottish Junior Cup ties away from the village. Funding was secured for improvements in 1975 and a new fence and pavilion were constructed at that time.

Entering from the car park, the only spectator facilities are in the pavilion immediately to the left. Refreshments are available from a kitchen which provides the only cover available for fans. The fact that you cannot see the pitch may be something of an advantage given Steelend's results over the years.

The remainder of the ground is flat grass and moss enclosed by a stockade-style fence. Given the 'frontier-like' location it is not hard to imagine being inside a Wild West stockade trying to repel the natives, not that many venture close to Woodside Park.

Back in the 1950s the ground was closed several times due to weather damage. Significant improvements were made in the 1970s with the current pavilion being opened in 1975/6.

SUPPORT
Steelend have a hardy dozen or so who never miss a home game and a few of them travel away as well. The recruitment of a younger team has generated some interest amongst their friends and relatives.

GETTING THERE
Car is the only sensible option. A mineral railway used to serve the mines in the hills above Woodside Park but the nearest railway station was three miles away in Oakley. Today the closest is Dunfermline which is eight miles from the village. The Number 75 Bus links Dunfermline and Steelend on an hourly basis.

This really is the middle of nowhere. Some potential visitors might know where Knockhill Motor Racing circuit is – if so then Steelend is close to there. From the M90 motorway exit at Junction 4 and follow the signs for Dollar. After about 6 miles you will approach Steelend and the football ground is the first thing you see on the right.

From the Kincardine Bridge take the A977 towards Kinross. At the Gartarry roundabout take the A907 towards Dunfermline. At the bottom of the dip in Comrie turn left onto the unclassified road to Saline. In Saline turn right and Woodside Park is about three-quarters of a mile away on the left.

PROGRAMMES
Although a board outside the ground suggests that programmes are on sale, this is unlikely to be the case. Steelend did produce them on a semi-regular basis back in the early 2000s but their only programme since then was for a Friendly against Celtic a few years back.

WEBSITE
Steelend have not enjoyed an active website for some years now.

TEN YEAR LEAGUE RECORD
1996/7	Fife League	14th out of 15	8pts
1997/8	Fife League	15th out of 15	13pts
1998/9	Fife League	15th out of 16	11pts
1999/00	Fife League	15th out of 15	2pts
2000/1	Fife League	15th out of 15	5pts
2001/2	Fife League	14th out of 15	13pts
2002/3	Fife League	8th out of 12	25pts
2003/4	Fife League	10th out of 10	8pts
2004/5	Fife League	11th out of 12	14pts
2005/6	Fife League	13th out of 13	14pts

TOWN (Population circa 400)
There really is very little to the settlement of Steelend. First mention of a farm of that name comes in the 19th Century and mine workings, both for coal and iron ore, were established around that time. A mineral railway from Dunfermline served the Saline Valley collieries and the Lethans Collieries and by the 1920s there was a Goods Yard called 'Steelend Goods'. Immediately after World War One a scheme of Council Housing was built at Steelend which remains the entirety of the village today. These houses were intended to be for the local miners and to replace sub-standard dwellings closer to the pits themselves that had been opened by the Wilson and Clyde Company. Steelend is adjacent to Saline which is larger and has more amenities although it is still no more than a large village.

SCOTTISH JUNIOR CUP RECORD			
95/6	Rd 1	Bye	
	Rd 2 H	West Calder United	2-5
96/7	Rd 1 A	Saltcoats Victoria	0-3
97/8	Rd 1	Bye	
	Rd 2 H	Forth Wanderers	0-4
98/9	Rd 1 H	Stoneyburn	1-8
99/0	Rd 1	Bye	
	Rd 2 H	Harthill Royal	2-3
00/1	Rd 1	Bye	
	Rd 2 A	Renfrew	0-4
01/2	Rd 1	Bye	
	Rd 2 H	Stonehouse Violet	1-2
02/3	Rd 1	Bye	
	Rd 2 A	Stoneyburn	3-2
	Rd 3 A	Shettleston	0-3
03/4	Rd 1	Bye	
	Rd 2 A	Johnstone Burgh	0-8
04/5	Rd 1	Bye	
	Rd 2 H	Dunbar United	1-2
05/6	Rd 1	Bye	
	Rd 2 A	Dyce	2-0
	Rd 3 A	Bo'ness United	0-5
06/7	Rd 1 H	Cumnock	2-3

HONOURS	
Fife County League	1950/1
Fife Cup	1946/7
Mitchell Cup	1950/1

THORNTON HIBS

Ground— Memorial Park
Ground Phone Number—
Postcode / GPS Location—KY1 4AN

Club Colours— Green and White

Club Secretary 2006/7— Audrey MacDonald, 01592 631135

Thornton lies midway between Glenrothes and Kirkcaldy. Unlike most places hosting a Fife Junior side, coal was not always the main industry and the inspiration for the junior football side – Thornton Hibs have been associated more with the railways than with mining.

HISTORY
Thornton Hibs began life as a juvenile side in 1913. They turned junior in 1935. They had always played in the public park and when they rose to the junior ranks they chose to stay put - improvements to the pavilion were made but that was all. The public park was renamed 'Memorial Park' in 1936 - possibly to recognise the death of King George V.

Thornton's finest achievement was reaching the Semi Final of the Scottish Junior Cup in 1960. They pulled in good crowds including an attendance of over 6000 for the match against Blantyre Celtic. Extra fencing was built to enclose the ground for this game and a 500-seater grandstand was hired from the Cupar Highland Games Society. Further temporary bench seating was provided for another 2000 spectators. Thornton's home advantage helped them to a 3-1 win. Their Semi Final was an all-Fife affair against St Andrews United which drew a crowd of 15411 to Raith Rovers ground in Kirkcaldy. Despite losing two players to injury during the game, Hibs held out for a 1-1 draw, despite playing the closing stages with 9 men. Hibs efforts were a telling factor in the replay which St Andrews won 2-1 in front of 10,000, again at Stark's Park.

Thornton were always forward-thinking and they installed a floodlight system in 1964. They played some competitive games under the lights but junior football has always been resistant to the concept of floodlit competition.

Gradually the club slipped back from prominence. Their Scottish Cup runs became less frequent an even success in local competitions was hard to come by. They did exceptionally well to win the Fife League in 2004 and qualified for the East Super League. However, they found the standard difficult to cope with and were relegated back into the Fife League after just one season.

Once again they found it difficult to adjust and by midway through the season they were struggling. The inevitable change of management followed but with little impact on results. Thornton's recent experience, going from

Super League to Central league strugglers, is typical of their topsy-turvy history.

GROUND
Memorial Park lies within a larger public park and struggles to call itself an enclosed football ground. Thankfully there have been no repetitions of the incident that led to the abandonment of a match against Dunnikier Colliery in January 1939 when an area of several square metres collapsed down an old mine shaft.

The long covered enclosure that existed on the north side of the ground has been demolished and replaced with a much smaller structure. Other than that there is simply grassed flat standing around the pitch. Committee men take entrance money at the park gates although the determined Scrooge would have no problem is finding alternative points of access.

SUPPORT
Thornton have a hard core home support of a few dozen.

GETTING THERE
Glenrothes and Thornton station is in Thornton, not Glenrothes. It is served by Fife Circle trains from Edinburgh. Located at the furthest point on the Circle, it makes little difference if passengers use the Dunfermline and Cowdenbeath trains or the Kirkcaldy ones. Perhaps it would be best to go one way and return the other to get the full panorama of scenic Fife.

By road Thornton will probably be approached along the A92 from Dunfermline or Dundee. From the south, follow Thornton signs from the large roundabout near Kirkcaldy. From the north Thornton is signposted from the large roundabout on the edge of Glenrothes, although you should be aware that this follows a very circuitous route.

Once in Thornton the Memorial Park is adjacent to the east side of the main road, in the centre of the village.

PROGRAMMES
Thornton produced a programme for their 1960 Scottish Junior Cup tie against Blantyre Vics. It was very unusual for Junior clubs to issue in those days. Made up of eight pages, and costing a hefty 6d, it doubled as a raffle ticket with five prizes of £1. The club also produced programme sin the mid to late 1990s, sometimes combined with a magazine about local history. These had ceased by the mid 2000s although programmes were still on sale at some games.

WEBSITE
The club have an active website at:
http://www.thornton-hibs.co.uk/

TEN YEAR LEAGUE RECORD
1996/7   Fife League   5th out of 15   33pts
1997/8   Fife League   7th out of 15   44pts

1998/9	Fife League	4th out of 16	59pts	
1999/00	Fife League	3rd out of 15	64pts	
2000/1	Fife League	6th out of 15	52pts	
2001/2	Fife League	4th out of 15	56pts	
2002/3	Fife League	2nd out of 12	54pts	
2003/4	Fife League	1st out of 10	40pts	Promoted
2004/5	East Super Leag	12th out of 12	16pts	Relegated
2005/6	Fife League	8th out of 13	36pts	

TOWN (Population 1900)

Thornton first appeared on maps around 1750. Thornton's growth really dates from 1848 when a major railway junction was created. Thornton was at the centre of a 'railway crossroads'. The main line north from Edinburgh to Dundee was bisected by a line from Cowdenbeath and Lochgelly to the west and to Levenmouth to the east. Thornton grew into a milling, mining and railway town with an Engine Shed. The latter developed into one of the main steam railway depots for Scotland and it was the base for the Permanent-Way Gangs serving the whole of Fife. During World War Two an armoured train was based at Thornton to protect the Forth and Tay railway crossings.

In the mid 1950s the National Coal Board planned and built the massive

Then and now—the former covered side is now a shadow of itself, with a smaller cover attached to the wall of the pavilion.

Memorial Park has lost some of its charm with this change—but it remains difficult to envisage how big crowds once attended here.

SCOTTISH JUNIOR CUP RECORD				
88/9	Rd 1	A	Coupar Angus	4-1
	Rd 2	A	Islavale	1-3
89/90	Rd 1	H	Cumnock	1-2
90/1	Rd 1	Bye		
	Rd 2	A	Stoneywood	1-5
91/2	Rd 1	H	Cambuslang Rangers	0-2
92/3	Rd 1	Bye		
	Rd 2	H	Yoker Athletic	0-1
93/4	Rd 1	A	Johnstone Burgh	0-2
94/5	Rd 1	Bye		
	Rd 2	H	Bankfoot Athletic	2-8
95/6	Rd 1	Bye		
	Rd 2	A	Sunnybank	0-4
96/7	Rd 1	Bye		
	Rd 2	H	Hill of Beath Hawthorn	0-3
97/8	Rd 1	A	Dalry Thistle	0-0
	Rep	H	Dalry Thistle	0-1
98/9	Rd 1	Bye		
	Rd 2	H	Maryhill	0-1
99/0	Rd 1	Bye		
	Rd 2	A	Bathgate Thistle	2-2
	Rep	H	Bathgate Thistle	1-1, 6-5 on pens
	Rd 3	H	Arthurlie	1-1
	Rep	A	Arthurlie	3-2
	Rd 4	A	Tranent	1-0
	Rd 5	A	Lanark United	0-2
00/1	Rd 1	Bye		
	Rd 2	A	Baillieston	5-2
	Rd 3	H	Dalry Thistle	3-1
	Rd 4	H	Carnoustie Panmure	0-1
01/2	Rd 1	Bye		
	Rd 2	A	Dundee Violet	0-3
02/3	Rd 1	A	Edinburgh United	2-2
	Rep	H	Edinburgh United	2-4
03/4	Rd 1	Bye		
	Rd 2	H	Rutherglen Glencairn	1-2
04/5	Rd 1	H	Lesmahagow	2-3
05/6	Rd 1	H	Bathgate Thistle	0-3
06/7	Rd 1	Bye		
	Rd 2	H	Dundonald Bluebell	1-7

HONOURS	
Fife County League (East)	1937/8
Fife County League	1952/3, 1958/9
Fife Regional League	1968/9
East Region Fife District League	2003/4
Fife Cup	1935/6, 1958/9, 1974/5, 1996/7, 1998/9
Cowdenbeath Cup	1938/9, 1959/60, 1962/3
East Fife Cup	1937/8, 1967/8, 1968/9
Fife Dryborough Cup	1977/8
Mitchell Cup	1951/2, 1958/9, 1959/60
West Fife Cup	1951/2, 1959/60

Rothes Mine close to Thornton. The neighbouring New Town of Glenrothes was envisaged as housing the workforce. However, subsidence, flooding and geological difficulties made the new pit uneconomic and it closed in 1962. The massive towers for the winding gear remained in situ until 1993. Some of the NCB Offices still exist housing the headquarters of the Fife Fire and Rescue Service.

As well as the Junior football ground Thornton also has one of the few remaining small greyhound tracks in Scotland, which is a much better appointed stadium than the football ground.

BELOW—Welcome to Memorial Park

BURNTISLAND SHIPYARD

Ground— Recreation Ground (aka Kirkton Park)
Ground Phone Number—
Postcode / GPS Location—KY3 0HL

Club Colours— White and Black

Club Secretary 2006/7— Andrew Beveridge, 01592 872359

The 'Shippie' are one of very few Senior clubs to compete in the Scottish Cup who are not members of the Scottish League, Highland, East of Scotland or South of Scotland Leagues. As of 2006/7 only Golspie Sutherland, Glasgow University and Girvan fell into the same category although at one time there were many such clubs. Scotland had a few of these 'works' teams although they were more prevalent in England. Babcock and Wilcox (from Renfrew) were SFA members until comparatively recently, whilst Lewis United (from Aberdeen) continue to play in the North Juniors.

HISTORY

During late Victorian times the top football side in Burntisland was Burntisland Thistle. However, they did not develop and by the early 20th Century they had slipped out of senior football. Burntisland Shipyard Amateurs were founded in 1923 and played in the Lothian Amateur League. The club was one of many in Scotland that served the needs of the workforce in a major industry. The shipyard in Burntisland was the major employer in the town and their Recreation section was meant to provide leisure opportunities for the workers and their families. For a brief spell in the late 1920s Shipyard moved to the Junior ranks but they quickly returned to the Amateurs. For 1931/2 Shipyard joined the Fife Football Association and the Edinburgh and District League. This was a senior league which included teams from Fife and the Lothians. Shipyard kept a reserve team in the Lothians League. Interest in the Edinburgh and District League quickly declined and within five years Shipyard were back in the Lothians Amateur League.

Unlike many others Shipyard retained their SFA membership. They had made their bow in the Scottish Cup in 1920/30, drawing 2-2 with Murrayfield Amateurs at Kirkton Park. The Shippie qualified for the Cup proper on various occasions during the 1930s but their biggest moment came in January 1939 when they were drawn at home to Celtic. Most teams in their position would have sold ground advantage (which was allowed in those days) but Shipyard stayed loyal and a crowd of around 3000 saw Celtic travel through and win 8-3.

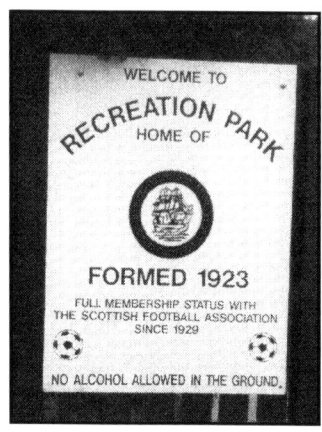

Shipyard workers hurriedly built a temporary six-row grandstand for this match.

After World War Two Shipyard moved from the Lothians League to the Fife Amateur League. They still kept their SFA membership but had very limited success in the Qualifying Cup. When the Burntisland Shipbuilding Company went into liquidation in 1969 the club were faced with closure. Bereft of their main sponsor the future looked bleak. However, their hard working committee kept the club afloat and they have continued to flourish since then. They switched from the Fife Amateur League, whose membership was dominated by clubs from North and East Fife, to the Kirkcaldy and District League. More recently they have joined the Kingdom Caledonian League.

Qualification for the Scottish Cup proper has become a rare event. In 1977/8 the Shipyard lost 4-1 at home to Berwick Rangers, but in 1994/5 they recorded a rare win. After a bye in Round One their opponents in Round Two were fellow non-league side St Cuthbert Wanderers. The 6-2 scoreline in Shipyard's favour put them into the hat with the 'big boys'. It was a disappointment to draw Highland League opposition in the shape of Huntly, away from home. Shipyard lost 7-0.

Despite their Amateur status, Shipyard have embraced a good youth development scheme. They enter a team in the SFA Youth Cup and have a reputation for bringing through their own young players

GROUND
The club have always played at the same venue although it has been known variously as Kirkton Park, Shipyard Recreation Ground and plain Recreation Ground. In the 1920s players stripped in the nearby George Hotel but by the 1930s an old railway carriage was sited behind the east goal and used for changing rooms. At one time the ground covered a much larger area and contained various other sporting facilities such as a bowling green and tennis courts. IN the Summer it was large enough to be used as a cricket field - all supported by the Shipyard's Recreation Fund. Kirkton Park was substantially upgraded in 1954. A new pavilion was built. The pitch was re-sown and re-aligned. A special match against Hearts was played on 8/5/1954 to 're-open' the ground. When the parent company went into liquidation the ground was sold to the local Education Board and subsequently passed to Fife Council. They sold off peripheral areas but retained an enclosed ground which allowed Shipyard to continue in the Qualifying Cup.

Entry is now made from the south side of the ground. As recently as the 1980s the original turnstiles still stood at the west corner of the ground but these have since been removed as more land was sold off.

On occasions Kirkcaldy YM played Scottish Junior Cup ties on the ground because their own field was not enclosed, notably in 1979/80 against Leven.

SUPPORT
A few dozen locals will regularly venture down to watch the Shipyard in action. For Qualifying Cup ties their numbers are increased considerably.

GETTING THERE
Burntisland is a fair distance from the motorway network. The easiest way to get there is by following the M90 to Junction 3 (Halbeath) and then taking the A92 towards Kirkcaldy. At the Burntisland turn-off follow the A909 down into the town. As you come into Burntisland turn right into Dollar Road - it's the first through road you can drive down after entering the town. Don't worry if you miss it - turn right at the roundabout at the foot of the road and then right again at Church Street to reach Dollar Road from the other end. The old entrance to the ground used to be in Glebe Street but it was knocked down to make way for new housing. There is a car park on the Dollar Road side of the ground.

Burntisland is well served by trains from Edinburgh. It is on the East Coast Main Line from Edinburgh to Aberdeen. You should note that not all the Aberdeen trains stop at Burntisland, but trains for Dundee, Markinch, Kirkcaldy and the Fife Circle do stop there. If taking a Fife Circle train then get one which is going anti-clockwise, via Kirkcaldy rather than clockwise via Dunfermline.

PROGRAMMES
Burntisland issued their first known programme for a match against Vale of Leithen in the Scottish Qualifying Cup of 1985/6. Since then they have often issued programmes for most home Qualifying Cup ties but not for other games. Of course they did also issue for the Scottish Cup match against St Cuthbert Wanderers in 1994.

WEBSITE
There is no website for Burntisland Shipyard FC.

TOWN (Population 8000)
Occupying a natural harbour, Burntisland is said to have been chosen by Agricola as a Roman naval base as early as AD 83. Given to Dunfermline Abbey in the 12th Century, a castle, church and 'kirkton' were established close to the harbour. The town was granted a royal charter by James V in 1541 and developed as a naval base and a port trading initially in fish and later in coal.

In 1850 the first rail ferry in the world, the Leviathan, came into operation, linking Burntisland and Granton on the opposite side of the Firth of Forth. It was the concept of Thomas Bouch who was later to be responsible for the design of the ill-fated Tay Railway Bridge. In addition to brewing and distilling, which was carried on from 1786 to 1916, Burntisland was a centre

SCOTTISH CUP RECORD				
29/30	Rd1	H	Murrayfield Ams	2-2
	Rep	A	Murrayfield Ams	0-2
33/4	Rd 1	A	Ross County	2-3
25/6	Rd 1	A	Dumbarton	2-4
38/9	Rd 1	H	Celtic	3-8
54/5	Rd 1	H	Forres Mechanics	1-7
55/6	Rd 1	A	Selkirk	2-3
56/7	Rd 1	A	Eyemouth United	2-3
71/2	Rd 1	H	Coldstream	2-0
	Rd 2	H	Elgin City	1-4
77/8	Rd 1	H	Berwick Rangers	1-4
94/5	Rd 1	Bye		
	Rd 2	H	St Cuthbert Wanderers	6-2
	Rd 3	A	Huntly	0-7

of ship building for half a century between 1918 and 1968 and an aluminium works, founded in 1917, closed in 2002. This added a layer of red bauxite dust to the town for many years.

Local landmarks include Rossend Castle which dates from the 12th century; the Burgh Chambers (1843); Burntisland Library and Museum; Mary Somerville's house (1595), once the home (1786-1817) of a daughter of one of Lord Nelson's captains and pioneer of women's education who gave her name to Oxford's first college for women founded in 1879; and the octagonal-towered St Columba's Church, said to be the first church built after the Reformation and where the General Assembly of the Church of Scotland, meeting in 1601, decided to publish the new authorised or 'King James' version of the Bible.

On the Binn Hill just above Burntisland James 'Paraffin' Young started shale oil production and founded a village in 1878.

Burntisland was a major holiday resort, popular with day trippers and longer-stayers from Edinburgh and Glasgow until the 1960s. Today it is just the day trippers who head for the Links - many of the Guest Houses and B and Bs have closed or provide DSS accommodation. Annual events in Burntisland include a Fair, Highland Games and the crowning of a 'Summer Queen' on the Links.

The pavilion sits behind the west goal at Shipyard's ground. The setting is more picturesque and much less maritime than might be expected from the club's name!

AMATEUR FOOTBALL 2006/7

KINGDOM CALEDONIAN FA

Three main Saturday Amateur leagues operate in this area. The Kingdom Caledonian FA is arguably the more 'senior' with teams of the highest standard. One member club, Fair City Athletic, comes from Perth and the remainder from Fife. The Fife Amateur FA and the Perthshire Amateur FA serve their respective areas with a fair turnover of teams from season to season.

The lists on this page indicate the home town of each club.

The Courier and Advertiser covers these leagues extensively although it would be necessary to get both the Perth and Fife editions for full details.

Balgonie Scotia	Coaltown of Balgonie
Ballingry Rovers	Glencraig
Bowhill Rovers	Bowhill
Burntisland Shipyard	Burntisland
Cowdenbeath Amateurs	Cowdenbeath
Cupar Hearts	Cupar
Eastvale	Buckhaven
Fair City Athletic	Perth
Kettle United	Kingskettle
Lomond Victoria	Falkland
Norton House	Leven
Rosyth Civil Service	Rosyth
Star Hearts	Star of Markinch
Strathmiglo United	Strathmiglo

FIFE AMATEUR FA

Auchtermuchty Bellevue	Auchtermuchty
Brucefield AFC	Dunfermline
Buckhaven Town	Buckhaven
Burntisland United	Burntisland
Camdean Athletic	Rosyth
CISWO AFC	Glenrothes
Dalgerty Bay AFC	Dalgety Bay
Denbeath AFC	Methil
Dysart AFC	Dysart (Kirkcaldy)
Fife Thistle	St Andrews
Freuchie AFC	Freuchie
Glenrothes AFC	Glenrothes
Glenvale AFC	Glenrothes
Greyhound Bar AFC	Oakley
Hill of Beath Ramblers	Hill of Beath
Inverkeithing Hillend Swifts	Inverkeithing
Inverkeithing Swifts	Inverkeithing
Kennoway	Kennoway
Kinghorn St Leonards	Kinghorn
Kirkland AFC	Methil
Kitty's AFC	Kirkcaldy
Leven United AFC	Leven
Lochgelly United	Lochgelly
Lumphinnans United	Lumphinnans
Markinch AFC	Markinch
Methilhill Strollers	Methilhill
Milton Violet	Milton of Balgonie
Newburgh Juveniles	Newburgh
Newtownglen AFC	Glenrothes
North East Saints AFC	Cupar
Pitlessie AFC	Pitlessie
Pittenweem Rovers	Piitenweem
Queensferry Albert	North Queensferry
Railway AFC	Methilhill
Roadhouse AFC	Kirkcaldy
Rosyth AFC	Rosyth
Springfield Rovers	Springfield
St Andrews AFC	St Andrews
St Andrews University	St Andrews
St Monans Swallows	St Monans
Townhill	Dunfermline
United Colleges AFC	St Andrews
Valleyfield AFC	Valleyfield

PERTHSHIRE AFA

Alyth AFC	Alyth
Auchterarder Primrose	Auchterarder
Ballinluig	Ballinluig
Balmoral United	Blairgowrie
Breadalbane AFC	Aberfeldy
Bridge of Earn AFC	Bridge of Earn
Bridgeton United	Almondbank
Burrelton Rovers	Burrelton
Comrie Rovers	Comrie (P&K)
Coupar Angus AFC	Coupar Angus
Fairfield United	Perth
Gateway AFC	Perth
Guildtown AFC	Guildtown
Kettins AFC	Kettins
Kinross United	Kinross
Kinrossie CSSA	Kinrossie
Letham AFC	Perth
Letham United	Perth
Meigle Vics	Meigle
Methven AFC	Methven
Murray Royal AFC	Scone
Newtyle Hearts	Newtyle
Perth Royale AFC	Perth
Rattray AFC	Rattray
Roselea AFC	Perth
Scone AFC	Scone
St Johns AFC	Perth
Stanley / Dunkeld CSSA	Stanley
Star of Atholl	Blair Atholl
Strathearn Grove	Crieff
Strathmore Albion	Blairgowrie
Tay Thistle	Perth
Vale of Atholl	Pitlochry
Vale of Earn	Crieff
Wolfhill AFC	Wolfhill

SUMMARY OF JUNIOR COMPETITIONS

Craig Stephen Cup (1974/5 - 1985/6)
For members of the Tayside JFA

Constitutional Cup (1920/1-1968/9)
Also known as the Perthshire Junior Consolation Cup

Cowdenbeath Cup (later the Bardon Aggregates Cup and the Interbew Cup) (1886/7-date)

Currie Cup (1910-11 - date) (Sponsors names include Whyte and Mackay Cup, Findlay and Co Cup) Open to Perthshire Junior clubs 1910/11 until 1967/8, then to all Tayside JFA clubs)

Downfield SC Cup (1992/3-2001/2)
Open to lower division Tayside JFA Clubs

East Coast Windows Cup

East Fife Cup (1894/5 - 1972/3)
Also known as the Montrave Cup

East Region Fife District League (2002/3 - 2005/6)
Following the creation of the East Region Superleague in 2002 the Fife League came fully under the auspices of the East JFA. The Champions were automatically promoted to the Superleague for the following season.

East Region Tayside District League
Following the creation of the East Region Superleague in 2002 the Tayside League came fully under the auspices of the East JFA. The Champions of the Premier Division were automatically promoted to the Superleague for the following season.

Express Cup (1958/9-1966/7)
For members of the Fife Junior FA

Fife and Lothians Cup (1968/9 - date)
Sponsors names include Charlie Bain Cup, Radio Forth Cup and the Heineken Cup)

Fife County League (1913/14-1967/8)
For a few seasons just before the Second World War the league was divided into East and West divisions.

Fife Cup
Sponsors names include the Peddie Smith Maloco Cup

Fife Dryborough Cup (1973/4-1985/6)
Dryborough's Brewers sponsored Cup competitions in the different Junior regions. The winners of these then played in a National Dryborough Competition on a semi-regular basis.

Fife Regional League (1968/9-2001/2)
The main league competition between these years for Fife clubs. In 1978/9 and 1979/80 it was divided into a First and Second Division.

Fife Shield (1893/4-1932/33)
Also known as the Dunfermline Shield

Fife-Tayside Cup (1995/6 - date)
Sponsors names include the Taycars Trophy and the Redwood Leisure Cup.

Herschell Trophy (1981/2 - date)
Played for by the winners of the previous season's Tayside League's two divisions. All proceeds go to Charity.

Kingdom Kegs Cup (1996/7 - date)
Sponsors names include the Stella Artois Cup and the Whitbread Trophy

John Masson Cup (1973/4 - 1974/5)

Laidlaw Shield (1979/80-1982/3)
For Fife Junior FA clubs

Martin-White Cup (1893/4-1938/9)
For clubs in the East Fife Junior FA

Midland Junior League (1939/40-1946/7)
Wartime competition for Junior clubs in Perthshire, Dundee and Angus

Mitchell Cup (1937/8-1966/7)
For members of the Fife Junior FA. Sometimes known as the Fife League Cup and sometimes as the Fife Consolation Cup.

PA Cup (1928/9-1972/3)
Presented by the Perthshire Advertiser and competed for by Perthshire Junior clubs.

Perthshire Junior Charity Cup (1905/6 - 1941/2)

Perthshire Junior Cup (1901/2-1972/3)

Perthshire Junior League (1899/00-1968/9)

Perthshire Rosebowl (1948/9 - 1968/9)

Red House Hotel Cup (1987/8-date)
Other sponsors name include the Rosebank CC Cup, Intersport Cup and Tay Land Rover Cup. From 1995/6 this competition was for Tayside Division 2 clubs)

St Johnstone YM Cup (1961/2 - 1967/8)

Scottish Junior Cup (1886/7 - date)

Tayside Dryborough Cup (1973/4 - 1986/7)

Tayside Regional League Cup (1968/9 - 1987/8)

Tayside Regional League Division 1 (1969/70 - 2001/2)

Tayside Regional League Division 2 (1969/70 - 1971/2)

West Fife Cup (1892/3 - 1972/3)
Also known as the Dunfermline Cup

Winter Cup (1977/8-1994/5)
Also known as the Inveralmond Cup. Competed for by Tayside Division 2 clubs.